Permanent Exhibition Guide Book of the Gyeongju National Museum

History and Culture of Silla

GYEONGJU NATIONAL MUSEUM

Notes to Readers

1. This book serves as the official guide book to the permanent exhibition of the Gyeongju National Museum.
2. The content is organized by period and theme, focusing on the museum's collection, to comprehensively convey the full history and culture of Silla.
3. The English text has been translated from the original Korean edition, with Chinese characters included where appropriate.
4. In the image captions, information is listed in the following order: name of artifact, excavation site, period, dimensions (cm), and National Heritage designation.
5. All of the featured artifacts are from the collections of Gyeongju National Museum or the National Museum of Korea, unless otherwise noted.
6. To provide the most comprehensive coverage, the guide book may include some items that are not currently on display.
7. Exhibition contents are subject to change due to inclusion in special exhibitions or scheduled rotation.
8. Display locations are noted in the list of plates as follows.

Silla History Exhibition Hall — Silla Art Exhibition Hall — Wolji Exhibition Hall — Outdoor Exhibition

Publication of the New Permanent Exhibition Guide Book

Gyeongju National Museum is pleased to introduce *The History and Culture of Silla*, a comprehensive new guide book of our permanent exhibition. Published in 2025, this guide book acts as the new face of the museum, as well as a friendly and insightful companion for visitors eager to deepen their knowledge of the collection. It has been ten years since the previous edition, a gap that prompted us to reflect on how to present the museum in its best light and engage meaningfully with our audience.

While somewhat overdue, the new volume is the first to incorporate the achievements of the recently renovated Silla History Exhibition Hall and Silla Art Exhibition Hall. Significantly, the guide book is organized chronologically, covering the full arc of Silla history with special focus on certain key themes. As such, it moves beyond the scope of previous guide books based primarily on exhibitions, such as *Silla History Exhibition Hall* (2021) and *Silla Art Exhibition Hall Guide* (2024), *Woiji Exhibition Hall Guide* (2025) fulfilling the long-standing requests for a permanent exhibition guide book, with a more integrative format.

With its broader chronological approach, which still remains grounded in the exhibited artifacts, we anticipate that this guide book will remain the representative publication of Gyeongju National Museum for many years, even as various displays are updated or reorganized. In addition, both the content and structure have been thoughtfully diversified to provide visitors with in-depth historical information while also nurturing their appreciation for the cultural heritage of Silla as art in its own right.

Museums are often seen as guardians of the past, but they also serve the present while looking ahead to the future. We hope that our visitors will experience and enjoy the museum as a vibrant, progressive space that grows with the times. May this guide book serve as a valuable companion to all those who care for and cherish the Gyeongju National Museum!

Director, Gyeongju National Museum

CONTENTS

I.

Prehistoric Times (Before Silla)

Evidence of human habitation in the Yeongnam region, where the Silla Kingdom would later arise, dates back to the Upper Paleolithic Period (approximately 40,000 to 10,000 years ago). Paleolithic people made and used chipped stone tools and lived by hunting and gathering. But around 10,000 years ago, in conjunction with global climate changes, humanity began to adopt a new agricultural way of life, marking the beginning of the Neolithic Period. As they began farming and cultivating their own food resources, Neolithic people gradually settled in one place, forming village communities and developing stone tool-making technologies to create various farming implements.

In the ensuing Bronze Age, which began around the fifteenth century BCE, various bronze objects appeared, such as bronze daggers and bronze mirrors, which were likely used as symbols of status and authority. Even so, stone tools continued to play a major role in many aspects of everyday life. Techniques for making stone tools became increasingly sophisticated, yielding a wider range of stone tools for farming and woodworking. The overall society of the Bronze Age also showed increasing complexity, as the full-scale farming of rice led to the emergence of social stratification and inequality. As more conflicts over land occurred between villages and groups, rulers and institutions of power that could mediate such conflicts began to appear. Clear evidence of these social transformations and the rise of a ruling class has been found at various sites of large settlements, as well as in the ditches surrounding these settlements and massive dolmen tombs. These Bronze Age developments laid the foundation for the rise of the earliest states.

Earliest Human Traces

Humans first began to use fire and make tools during the Paleolithic Period, which spans from approximately 2.5 million years to about 10,000 years ago. Over these millions of years, dramatic environmental changes occurred, including repeated glacial and interglacial periods. Early humans of the time lived in small groups and moved from place to place in search of food, which they obtained by hunting and gathering. Their temporary dwellings consisted mainly of caves or rock shelters near rivers or streams. Paleolithic people would have crafted tools from stone, wood, animal bones, and antlers, but for the most part, only the stone tools have survived. In the earlier Paleolithic, large stone tools such as handaxes and polyhedrons were predominantly used. Moving into the later Paleolithic, smaller and more refined tools (such as scrapers, burins, and tanged points) were developed to serve specific purposes.

Homo erectus is estimated to have appeared in East Asia around 1.5 million years ago. In the Korean Peninsula, however, the earliest evidence of human existence yet discovered is *Homo sapiens* from the Middle Pleistocene period (about 780,000–130,000 years ago). Most archaeological sites in the Yeongnam region, which includes Gyeongju, the center of the Silla Kingdom, date to the Upper Paleolithic Period. Representative examples include the Sinhwa-ri site in Ulsan and the Sanseo-ri site in Pohang. These findings suggest that the Gyeongju area was also likely inhabited from the Upper Paleolithic Period.

Development of Tools

Stone tools from the Paleolithic Period were primarily used for hunting and gathering. They were made by chipping stones to obtain a desired edge or shape, and can be distinguished from naturally broken rocks by the presence of deliberate strike marks. Various techniques were used to detach stone flakes, including direct percussion, in which the core was struck directly with a stone hammer; indirect percussion, in which a wedge was used to detach flakes; and pressure flaking, in which a tool was pressed against the core to remove flakes. Blade technology emerged in the Upper Paleolithic, with wedges being used to remove elongated flakes (blades) from cores, making it easier to produce scrapers, burins, notched blades, and serrated blades. Toward the end of the Paleolithic, grinding techniques began to appear, allowing for more refined surface processing of stone tools.

001
Pick
Maae-ri, Andong
Paleolithic Period
L. 23.6 cm

002
Chopping Tools
Maae-ri, Andong
Paleolithic Period
L. 13.9 cm (left)

003
Stone Hammers
Maae-ri, Andong
Paleolithic Period
L. 14.4 cm (far left)

004
Blades, Core

Sinhwa-ri, Ulsan · Sanseo-ri, Pohang
Paleolithic Period
L. 6.7 cm (far right)
Gyeongju National Museum, Ulsan Museum

005
Refitted Stone Tools

Sinhwa-ri, Ulsan
Paleolithic Period
L. 8.4-10.8 cm (bottom left)
Ulsan Museum

In the Upper Paleolithic, various stone tools were made from flakes that had been chipped off of larger stone cores. Notably, both stone flakes and the cores from which they had been removed were found together at the Sinhwa-ri site in Ulsan. By refitting the flakes back onto the cores, researchers were able to study the specific ways in which the cores were struck to make the stone tools.

Dawn of a New Era

Around 10,000 years ago, the last Ice Age came to an end. As the global climate warmed, human life and culture changed dramatically, marking the end of the Paleolithic Period and the beginning of the Neolithic Period. Defining aspects of the Neolithic Period include the advent of agriculture and a more sedentary lifestyle, as well as the emergence of pottery and ground stone tools. With the beginning of agriculture, humans were no longer fully dependent on nature, entering a new stage in which they actively utilized and modified their environment. With the increasing demand for farming tools to cultivate land and harvest crops, the technology for producing stone tools significantly advanced, resulting in a wider variety of tool types and functions.

The rise of agriculture also encouraged a more sedentary way of life, as Neolithic people began to settle in communities, usually near rivers or in coastal areas. This new lifestyle triggered another revolutionary cultural milestone of this period: the invention of pottery. For people living a nomadic existence, large and heavy ceramic vessels were impractical compared to containers made from leather or fibers. But pottery was extremely useful in a sedentary lifestyle, particularly since it allowed for cooking. The use of pottery expanded the range of edible foods and the diversity of cooking methods, which greatly improved the nutritional intake of Neolithic people.

A number of important Neolithic sites have been uncovered and excavated in Gyeongju and its surrounding regions. These include the site in Bonggil-ri, Gyeongju, where the remains of pit dwellings were found, and a shell midden in Sejuk-ri, Ulsan, which contained refuse from daily life. In Uljin, a burial containing the remains of numerous individuals was discovered in Hupo-ri, while the coastal site of Jukbyeon-ri yielded the oldest known fragments of a boat ever found in Korea, along with a wooden object presumed to be an oar.

New Subsistence Economy and Advancement of Stone Tool Technology

As global temperatures started to rise around 10,000 years ago, sea levels increased, and humans began to actively utilize marine resources. Neolithic people developed new tools and methods for fishing in rivers and the sea. They ventured into deeper waters by boat, where they used harpoons and composite fishing hooks to catch large marine animals, including whales and sharks. They also gathered shellfish and aquatic plants for subsistence. At the same time, early agriculture began, focusing on grains that were relatively easy to cultivate, such as foxtail millet, barnyard millet, and proso millet.

Whereas Paleolithic tools were made simply by striking a stone core with stone or bone, the Neolithic Period saw the widespread use of grinding techniques to shape tools and sharpen their edges. Such techniques were used to produce various implements for the new practice of farming, including hoes, ploughshares, sickles, and axes, as well as bone tools and ornaments. At the Jukbyeon-ri site in Uljin, archaeologists discovered the raw stone materials used to make ground stone tools, as well as cutting tools, grindstones, and hammerstones, providing valuable insights into how Neolithic people manufactured stone tools.

006
Stone Harpoons
Jukbyeon-ri, Uljin
Neolithic Period
L. 9.9 cm (right)

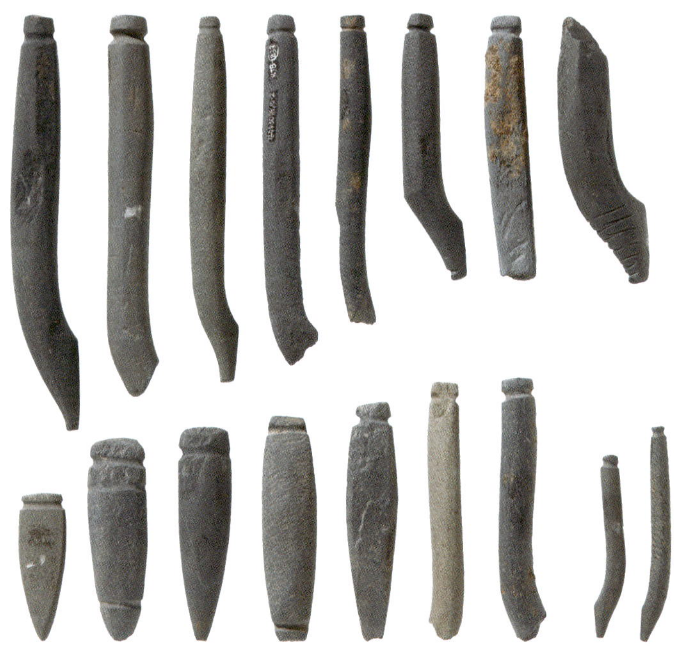

007
Fishing Hooks
Jukbyeon-ri, Uljin
Neolithic Period
L. 13.0 cm (top left)

008
Stone Digging Tools

Jukbyeon-ri, Uljin
Neolithic Period
L. 20.3 cm (right)

009
Various Types of Stone Tools

Bonggil-ri, Gyeongju ·
Jukbyeon-ri, Uljin
Neolithic Period
L. 11.5 cm (far right)

010

Oar

Jukbyeon-ri, Uljin
Neolithic Period
L. 170.0 cm

A fragment of a boat and a wooden object presumed to be an oar were unearthed from the Neolithic cultural layer of the Jukbyeon-ri site in Uljin, located on the east coast. The boat is estimated to date to around 6,000 BCE, and is similar to another one discovered in Bibong-ri, Changnyeong, along the Nakdong River. Although the fragment is only about 50 cm long and 64 cm wide, it can be confirmed that the boat was made by hollowing out the log of a camphor tree. The oar, on the other hand, is made from oak and measures about about 170 cm in length with a trapezoidal section that would have been put into the water and pushed for propulsion.

011

Boat Fragment

Jukbyeon-ri, Uljin
Neolithic Period
W. 64.0 cm

Emergence of Pottery

One of the most important developments of the Neolithic Period was the invention of pottery, which enabled new cooking methods, such as boiling, blanching, and simmering, and thereby broadened the range of edible foods. Pottery also made it much easier to store and transport food. As access to food became more stable, people were able to settle in one place for longer periods, fostering the development of culture and the arts. The earliest pottery ever found on the Korean Peninsula consists of plain, undecorated ceramic vessels discovered on Jeju Island, which date to around 10,000 years ago. In the eastern and southern coastal regions, raised-design pottery and stamped pottery was popularly used around 8,000 years ago, while comb-pattern pottery became prevalent in the midwestern region around 6,500 years ago. Most Neolithic pottery is decorated with patterns across the entire surface, with the patterns gradually becoming simpler over time. In the Gyeongju area, raised-design pottery is more common than comb-pattern pottery, and red-colored pottery has also frequently been found, including at the Jukbyeon-ri site in Uljin.

012
Pottery
Bonggil-ri, Gyeongju · Songjuk-ri, Gimcheon · Jukbyeon-ri, Uljin
Neolithic Period
H. 42.6 cm (back row, right)

013
Comb-pattern Pottery
Songjuk-ri, Gimcheon
Neolithic Period
H. 35.0 cm

Comb-pattern pottery first emerged on the Korean Peninsula around 6,500 years ago, primarily in the midwestern region, before spreading rapidly across the entire peninsula around 5,500 years ago. Comb-pattern pottery vessels typically have pointed bases, and their surface is decorated with geometric patterns of dots and lines, for which they are named. Over time, these decorations became simpler and smaller, covering less of the surface. Comb-pattern pottery vessels show different shapes and decorations depending on the time period and place, allowing them to be roughly divided into four regions: midwest, south, east, and northwest. Comb-pattern pottery gradually dwindled over time until completely disappearing around 3,500 years ago, being replaced by the plain pottery of the Bronze Age.

Burials and Funerary Rites

Burials provide valuable insights into people's beliefs about death and the afterlife. Although no Paleolithic burials have yet been discovered on the Korean Peninsula, various types of Neolithic burials have been found. In most cases, the deceased were buried in pits dug into the ground, but burials in natural caves and human bones in pottery vessels have also been found. Although grave goods from Neolithic burials are generally sparse, items such as shell bracelets and anklets, jade ornaments, pottery, and stone tools were sometimes placed in graves for the deceased. In some cases, the deceased were covered with broken pieces of pottery or shells, suggesting that funerary rituals had taken place. At the Hupo-ri site in Uljin, archaeologists uncovered a large burial pit, about 4 meters in diameter that contained the remains of more than forty men and women, mostly in their twenties, along with tubular stone beads, ornaments, and more than 180 finely polished stone axes.

014
Ornaments
Hupo-ri, Uljin
Neolithic Period
L. 11.4 cm (far right)

015
Stone Axes
Hupo-ri, Uljin
Neolithic Period
L. 54.2 cm (far left)

Social Stratification and Emergence of Power

On the Korean Peninsula, the Bronze Age began around the fifteenth century BCE. During this period, the advancement of agriculture eventually led to intensified conflicts and disputes between villages over land and surplus production. Thus, individuals who could mediate such disputes or protect the community gradually emerged as social leaders, forming a new social class. This development is evidenced by the construction of large dolmens during the Bronze Age. Serving as both communal monuments and burials for powerful individuals, these stone structures clearly illustrate the newly stratified society of the time.

The complex social structures and economic developments of the Bronze Age eventually led to the emergence of Gojoseon, the first state in Korea, which arose in the northern part of the Korean Peninsula and the area of Liaoning (present-day China). Gojoseon was based on the foundations of the "*Bipa*-shaped Bronze Dagger Culture," which refers to a special type of dagger shaped like a *bipa* (Korean string instrument resembling a lute) and assembled using separate blade and hilt parts. Being distinct from either Chinese *dao*-style swords or bronze daggers of the northern Ordos culture, *bipa*-shaped bronze daggers have come to exemplify the unique nature of Korea's Bronze Age culture.

In the southern Korean Peninsula, there is little physical evidence of organized political systems from this period. However, some historical texts mention Jinguk, a polity that is believed to have been established by the third or second century BCE. While its exact nature remains unclear, Jinguk likely emerged from the stratified and economically advanced societies of the Bronze Age, and laid the foundations for the later societies of Samhan.

Development of Farming and Functional Diversification of Stone Tools

Farming became more widely established during the Bronze Age, with crops such as rice, millet, sorghum, soybeans, and barley being cultivated. The development of farming led to larger settled communities with increasing populations, which were typically established on the plains or low-lying hills near rivers, where both water and farmland were easy to access. These villages included residential areas, burial grounds, production facilities, communal spaces, ritual sites, and cultivated fields. They were sometimes surrounded by wooden palisades or circular ditches to protect against external threats.

In this period, the widespread use of wooden farming tools led to an increasing need for stone tools for woodworking, such as stone axes, adzes, plane blades, and chisels, the likes of which have been found across the Korean Peninsula. Stone tools were also employed for farming, with semi-lunar stone knives and stone sickles being used to harvest grain, and stone hoes, spades, and hand plows used to dig and till the soil. In addition to farming tools, stone weapons were also developed in the Bronze Age, including ground stone daggers and arrowheads. The presence of such weapons suggests that communal conflicts were occurring, likely over land ownership or the distribution of surplus goods.

016

Stone Axes

Gapsan-ri, Gyeongju · Joyang-dong, Gyeongju · Jinrali, Cheongdo
Bronze Age
L. 13.2 cm (left)

017

Stone Adzes

Seokjang-dong, Gyeongju · Sinpyeong-ri, Yeongdeok · Jinra-ri, Cheongdo
Bronze Age
L. 22.3 cm (top left)

018
Stone Sickles
Chunghyo-dong, Gyeongju · Yongjang-ri, Gyeongju · Sangan-dong, Ulsan
Bronze Age
L. 26.3 cm (top)

019
Stone Chisels
Gapsan-ri, Gyeongju · Seokjang-dong, Gyeongju
Bronze Age
L. 7.7 cm (left)

020
Various types of Stone Tools
Gyeongsang-do
Bronze Age
L. 13.8 cm (bottom right)

A wide variety of stone tools have been unearthed in Gyeongju, including ground stone daggers, axes, chisels, arrowheads, and semi-lunar stone knives. While this assemblage roughly matches the types of tools found in the surrounding area of Yeongnam, some artifacts are unique to Gyeongju. Of particular note is a "ㄱ"-shaped stone knife discovered at the Hwangseong-dong site in Gyeongju, which matches knives that have primarily been found along the east coast, from the Duman River region in the north to the southern coast. In addition, moon-shaped stone maces, which were likely used in rituals, were found in Gyeongju at both the Dongcheon-dong and Hwangseong-dong sites.

021
Semi-lunar Stone Knifes
Gyeongsangbuk-do
Bronze Age
L. 11.6 cm (center)

022
Red Burnished Pottery
Wolsan-ri, Gyeongju · Chunghyo-dong, Gyeongju · Cheongdo
Bronze Age
H. 13.9 cm (center)

023
Pottery
Gyeongsangbuk-do
Bronze Age
H. 58.2 cm
(back row, left)

Most pottery from the Bronze Age has no surface decorations. These plain pottery vessels were made from relatively coarse clay mixed with sand or rock fragments and fired in open pit kilns. However, some Bronze Age pottery is embellished with simple incised lines or perforations, or coated with either red or black pigment. Common vessel types include deep and shallow bowls, plates, large and small jars, and mounted vessels. These vessels can be categorized according to their respective function for cooking, storing, or serving food, or as grave goods.

Emergence of Rulers

The representative burial structures of the Bronze Age are dolmens, which signify the emergence of powerful rulers. The construction of dolmens, which involved moving huge stones weighing many tons, would have required substantial labor and organization, thus indicating the strong authority of those who oversaw and directed the process. The status and power of such rulers is further evidenced by grave goods, such as bronze daggers, ground stone daggers, and stone bead ornaments, as well as mace heads shaped like stars or the moon, which have been recovered from residential sites. Despite their imposing appearance, however, dolmens in the Yeongnam region have not yielded a wealth of grave goods, with most containing only a few items, such as ground stone daggers, red-burnished pottery, or arrowheads, either individually or in small quantities. This would seem to suggest that the rulers of the Yeongnam region sought to express their power and prestige via the monumental scale of the tomb itself, rather than through an abundance of luxurious grave goods. More than 100 dolmens are known to exist in Gyeongju, although relatively few have been excavated. Prominent or notable examples include the Gapsan-ri stone mound tomb and the dolmens of Seokjang-dong and Hwangseong-dong, which feature stone platforms delineating their burial precincts.

024
Ground Stone Dagger

Gaknam-myeon, Cheongdo
Bronze Age
L. 41.0 cm

One of the representative stone artifacts of the Bronze Age is the ground stone dagger, made by grinding pieces of slate or shale to create sharpened edges. These daggers can be broadly divided into two main types: those with hilts and those without. Some of the hilts have a horizontal groove in the center, while others do not. Ground stone daggers, especially those with a hilt with no groove, have primarily been discovered in burials. They have also occasionally been found at residential sites, in which case they usually have either no hilt or a hilt with a central groove. The daggers with no hilt typically have a tang at one end, where they were likely affixed to a wooden hilt.

025
***Bipa*-shaped Bronze Dagger**

Yejeon-ri, Cheongdo
Bronze Age
L. 34.8 cm

As the name indicates, "*bipa*-shaped bronze daggers" have a blade shaped like a *bipa*, which is an ancient string instrument resembling a lute. They have also sometimes been called "Liaoning-type bronze daggers," since they have often been found in the Liaoning region of northeast China, or "Gojoseon-type bronze daggers," since they are distinctive artifacts of Gojoseon. Their defining features include the broad, rounded lower blade and the sharp points on both sides near the middle of the blade. Significantly, their blade and hilt were made separately and then joined together, which distinguishes them from Chinese bronze daggers, which were typically cast as a single piece. This particular *bipa*-shaped bronze dagger was excavated from Yejeon-ri, Cheongdo, and closely resembles examples from the Shiertaiyingzi Culture in Chaoyang, Liaoning Province, China. The lack of a vertical groove in the tang indicates that this is one of the earliest *bipa*-shaped bronze daggers ever discovered in the Yeongnam region.

026

Stone Moon Mace

Doji-dong, Gyeongju · Dongcheon-dong, Gyeongju · Hwangseong-dong, Gyeongju · Gajaegol, Ulsan · Chogok-ri, Pohang
Bronze Age
D. 10.7 cm (top right)
Gyeongju National Museum,
Ulsan Museum

027

Ground Stone Daggers

Gyeongsangbuk-do
Bronze Age
L. 20.0 cm (far left)

028
Stone Arrowheads

Gyeongsangbuk-do
Bronze Age
L. 11.6 cm (botton left)

II.

Formation and Development of Saroguk

The Silla Kingdom originated as Saroguk, one of twelve small polities forming Jinhan, a loose confederacy in the southern Korean Peninsula, east of the Nakdong River. Saroguk was centered in the Gyeongju basin along the Hyeongsan River, where various settlements and villages had been established over time, using natural landmarks, such as mountains or streams, as boundaries. According to historical records, Saroguk was founded in 57 BCE when six of these villages united and chose Park Hyeokgeose (r. 57 BCE–4 CE) as their king. In addition to Park Hyeokgeose's clan, other immigrant groups such as the Seok and Kim clans also played major roles in the foundation of Saroguk. These clans likely included refugees from Gojoseon, who introduced advanced technologies and cooperated with the locals to establish Saroguk. The Park, Seok, and Kim clans established a rotational kingship system that defined the ruling power in early Saroguk.

Saroguk's development into an ancient state was facilitated by its geographical advantages as a transportation hub connecting the inland to the coast, along with its advanced technology for producing iron. The large-scale production and distribution of iron weapons and tools enhanced Saroguk's military strength, enabling them to conquer neighboring regions and expand their territory, as documented in *Samguk sagi* (*History of the Three Kingdoms*). One of the key archaeological indicators of Saroguk's expansion is the spread of Gyeongju-style wooden cist tombs, which feature a long, narrow main cist and an auxiliary cist within a single burial pit. Such tombs originated in Gyeongju, but have also been identified in surrounding regions such as Pohang, Ulsan, Gyeongsan, Daegu, and Chilgok, showing the widening spread of Saroguk's influence.

Emergence of Saroguk and New Cultural Elements

The rise of Saroguk is linked to the emergence of wooden coffin tombs in the Yeongnam region, which began to replace the dolmens of the Bronze Age starting around the second century BCE. After initially being used for individual burials, these tombs gradually began to form clusters, which were typically located along major transportation routes, suggesting the presence of large settlements. Grave goods found in these tombs, such as bronze artifacts, glass beads, and Yayoi pottery, provide evidence of exchange between communities, including interactions with distant lands like the Hoseo and Honam regions of western Korea, and even Kyushu, Japan. Such discoveries attest to the changing social conditions and economic practices of the time, which required a more centralized political structure uniting wider regions, beyond small villages, thus fostering the development of state-polities like Saroguk.

Representative sites of wooden coffin tomb clusters in Gyeongju include Joyang-dong, Tap-dong, Gujeong-dong, Sara-ri, and Hagu-ri. Unlike Bronze Age dolmens, these wooden coffin tombs were richly furnished with an abundance of elaborate grave goods, clearly intended to display the social status of the deceased. Notably, these grave goods include not only traditional prestige items, such as bronze artifacts, but also ironware, a new cultural element at the time, indicating the importance of iron technology in Saroguk's growth and development.

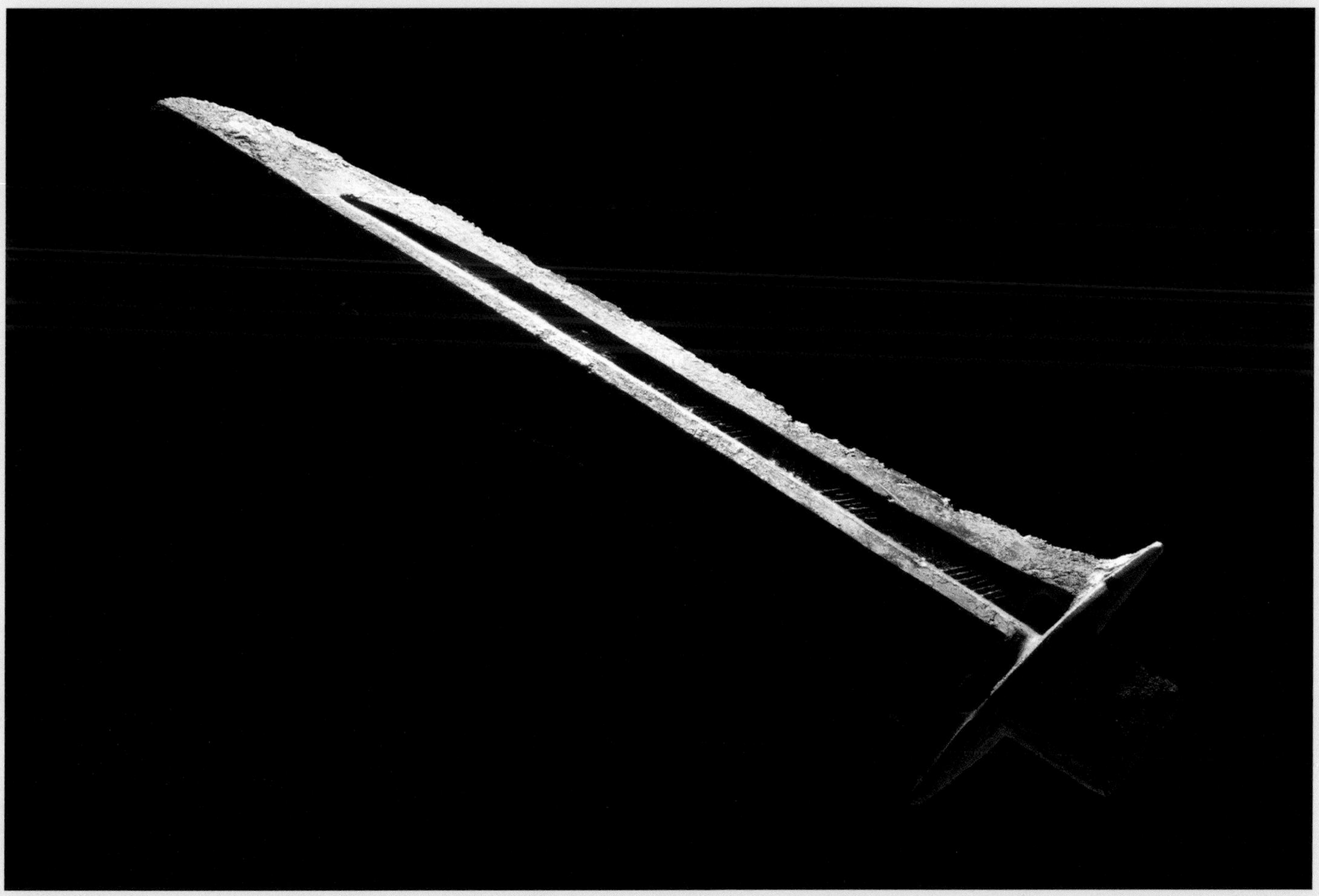

029
Slender Bronze Daggers

Gyeongsangbuk-do · Pyongyang
Early Iron Age–Proto Three Kingdoms Period
L. 31.5 cm (far right)

Slender bronze daggers first appeared in the midwestern region of the Korean Peninsula in the fifth to fourth century BCE. Like the *bipa*-shaped bronze daggers of early Gojoseon, from which they developed, slender bronze daggers also have a separate blade and hilt that were joined together. They are characterized by the concave indentations in the middle of the blade. While they are considered to be representative weapons of late Gojoseon, these daggers have also been found in wooden coffin tombs (some of which were packed with stones) in the Yeongnam region, indicating that they were used as grave goods during the early Iron Age. In Gyeongju, they have been found, albeit in limited quantities, in Ipsil-ri, Jukdong-ri, Sara-ri, and Tap-dong. Slender bronze daggers began to disappear around the start of the first century CE, gradually being replaced by iron swords.

030
Various Types of Bronze Artifacts

Gyeongsangbuk-do · Pyongyang
Early Iron Age-Proto Three Kingdoms Period
L. 51.3 cm (bottom left)

031

Bronze Artifacts

Jukdong-ri, Gyeongju
1st century BCE
L. 23.0 cm (slender bronze dagger)
Treasure
Gift of Lee Yang-sun

This collection of artifacts excavated from the Jukdong-ri site in Gyeongju represents the "Slender Bronze Dagger Culture" of the late Bronze Age. The artifacts include a dagger, spearhead, dagger-axe, dagger hilt decorations, pole bells, buttons, horse bells, and bit. Of particular note are the pole bells, a type of ornament that functions like a bell, which would have been attached to a pole or spear and shaken to make sounds during special rituals. The pole bells, which are typically found in pairs, have a hollow upper body containing bronze beads and a semi-circular ring at the bottom, which is likely where tassels or other decorative accessories were attached. The set also includes a number of bronze buttons, all of which have round eyelets on the back.

Reverse of Buttons

032

Bronze Mirrors

Joyang-dong, Gyeongju
1st century BCE
D. 8.0 cm (right)

While most of the bronze mirrors excavated from Saroguk sites follow the style of mirrors produced in China during the Western Han period, there are also some modified versions of Han mirrors that must have been indigenously produced. As opposed to earlier bronze mirrors with multiple knobs on the back, which symbolized religious authority, later bronze mirrors like these were typically used as grave goods representing the status and power of social leaders. For example, a bronze mirror in the style of the Western Han was excavated from Joyang-dong Tomb 38, showing the political and diplomatic authority of the Saroguk ruler who had led interactions with Nangnang (Lelang) Commandery.

033

Bronze Dagger-Axe Sheath and Iron Dagger-Axe

Yongjeon-ri, Yeongcheon
1st century BCE
L. 32.0 cm

This sheath was once used to hold an iron dagger-axe. The wooden parts of the sheath have disintegrated over time, leaving only the bronze frame intact. Similar bronze-framed dagger-axe sheaths have been discovered at various sites, including in Jisan-dong and Pyeongni-dong in Daegu. More recently, a lacquered dagger-axe sheath was unearthed from Wooden Coffin Burial 1 at Yangji-ri in Gyeongsan.

034

Bronze Crossbow Trigger Mechanism

Yongjeon-ri, Yeongcheon
1st century BCE
L. 8.3 cm

This is a firing mechanism for a mechanically enhanced bow from ancient times, which functioned like a crossbow. The discovery of components from such crossbows, which are called "*sweonoe*" or "*noh*" in Korean, is extremely rare. Historical records state that Silla possessed powerful crossbows, indicating that such weapons were widely used from the Three Kingdoms period onward. While such crossbows offered greater accuracy than traditional bows, they also took longer to load and re-fire.

Appearance of Iron and *Wajil* Pottery

The earliest elements of iron culture first emerged on the Korean Peninsula around the fourth to third century BCE, as a result of cultural interactions with the northeast regions of China. However, full-scale iron production did not begin in the southern regions of the Korean Peninsula until around the second century BCE. This historical context is supported by a passage in the "Biographies of the Dongyi" section from the "Book of Wei" in *Sanguozhi* (*Records of the Three Kingdoms*), which states, "Iron was produced in the lower Nakdong River region and exported to Nangnang (Lelang) and Wa (Japan)."

Wajil pottery was produced with new technology that arose in the southern part of the peninsula, influenced by grayish ware from China. Unlike undecorated pottery, which was made from coarse clay and fired in open kilns, resulting in its reddish color, *wajil* pottery was made from softer base material, similar to roof tiles, and fired in enclosed kilns at temperatures of 800 to 900°C, resulting in a gray or grayish-white color. *Wajil* pottery also tends to have a more uniform and symmetrical shape than earlier undecorated pottery, indicating that it was made with a turntable or simple wheel. Initially, *wajil* pottery was produced in roughly the same forms as traditional undecorated pottery, but new vessel types emerged over time, including mounted vessels and fitted lids.

035

Various Types of Iron Artifacts

Yongjeon-ri, Yeongcheon
1st century BCE
L. 48.0 cm (top)

A wooden coffin tomb in Yongjeon-ri, Yeongcheon, yielded a mixture of bronze objects, including a crossbow trigger, a spearhead, and a dagger-axe sheath, along with more than seventy iron artifacts, including axes, sickles, spearheads, a horse bit, a chisel, and an anchor-shaped object. Interestingly, twenty-five iron axes were laid out on the floor of the tomb, likely with the intent of displaying the high status of the deceased. The Yongjeon-ri site is contemporaneous to Tomb 38 of Joyang-dong (Gyeongju) and Tomb 1 of Daho-ri (Changwon) and is considered to be a key archaeological site representing the early iron culture of Saroguk.

• Sara-ri Tomb 130

Located on a low hill in Sara-ri, Seo-myeon, Gyeongju, Tomb 130 is a wooden coffin tomb dating to the first century CE. Along with a variety of iron artifacts, including a sword, the tomb also yielded a bronze dagger and four bronze mirrors following the style of Han mirrors. Both the bronze dagger and iron sword originally consisted of a blade, hilt, and lacquered scabbard, but the wooden parts of the scabbards have disintegrated, leaving only the fittings. The blade of the sword is made from iron, but the hilt and scabbard fittings are bronze. Based on this outstanding collection of grave goods, which ranks among the most impressive ever found in Korea, the occupant of this tomb is presumed to have been a ruler of Saroguk.

036
Sara-ri Tomb 130 Excavated Artifacts

Sara-ri Tomb 130, Gyeongju
1st century CE
L. 46.5 cm (lacquered scabbard for iron dagger)

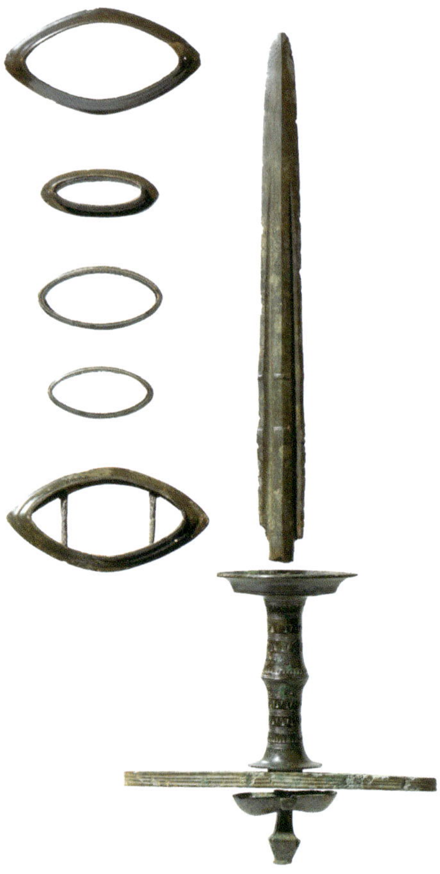

037

Slender Bronze Dagger and Scabbard Fittings

Sara-ri Tomb 130, Gyeongju
1st century CE
Restoration L. 56.8 cm (bronze dagger)

This is a slender bronze dagger of the early Iron Age, along with several metal fittings from its scabbard. While the wooden part of the scabbard has not survived, the fittings suggest that the scabbard had flared ends and a slightly concave center. The wooden surface of the scabbard was coated with lacquer, with the metal fittings added as additional decorations. Scabbards of this type have mainly been found in wooden coffin and stone-packed wooden coffin tombs around Pyongyang or in the southern regions of the Korean Peninsula. The placement of such an ornate object in a tomb was likely intended to convey the elite status of a Saroguk ruler.

038
***Wajil* Pottery**

Gyeongju
1st-4th century CE
H. 21.8 cm (front right)

039
Bird-shaped Pottery

Gyeongju
Three Kingdoms Period
H. 43.6 cm (back row, left)

Bird-shaped pottery vessels have frequently been found in tombs dating to the mid-third century throughout the region east of the Nakdong River, particularly at Saroguk sites. These vessels are hollow and have a large hole on the back, where they were probably filled with some type of liquid, and a smaller hole in the tail, where the liquid would have been poured out. Given that they have primarily been found in tombs or other burial sites, bird-shaped pottery vessels are believed to have been used in funerary rituals and then interred with the deceased, likely symbolizing the ancient spiritual beliefs of people who wished to ascend to the heavens after death.

Expansion of Iron Culture

One of the driving forces behind Saroguk's emergence as the leading polity of Jinhan was its advanced ironworking technology. From the late second to the third century CE, both the quality and quantity of Saroguk's iron implements drastically increased. The overall system for producing iron became more specialized and efficient, thanks to the division of labor, allowing for the mass production and standardization of a wider range of forged iron tools. The increasing availability of such tools boosted agricultural productivity, and also led to more trade and exchange involving iron. The commercial and economic importance of iron is documented in *Sanguozhi* (*Records of the Three Kingdoms*), in the "Paragraph on the Han" from the "Biographies of the Dongyi" in the "Book of Wei," which states that iron was used as a medium of exchange in Jinhan and Byeonhan.

One of the key archaeological indicators of this transition is the emergence of wooden cist tombs from the mid-second century onward. Compared to earlier wooden coffin tombs, wooden cist tombs have yielded significantly more iron artifacts, indicating that Saroguk had achieved a stable system of iron production and distribution. The production of superior iron weapons would have given Saroguk an important advantage in military conflicts and power struggles with neighboring polities.

Iron Production and Territorial Expansion

The spread of iron culture had a profound impact on agriculture and warfare. Iron farming tools allowed a person to cultivate a much wider area than in previous eras, significantly increasing agricultural yields. Meanwhile, the production of iron weapons and armor suggests the intensification of warfare during this period. Excavations at the Hwangseong-dong site in Gyeongju uncovered diverse archaeological evidence of sustained iron production from the first to the fourth century CE. The findings included traces of both casting (in which molten metal is poured into molds) and forging (heating iron ingots and hammering them into shape). Saroguk's advanced iron technology gave it a decisive military edge over rival polities. *Samguk sagi* records that, during the period when the rulers were referred to as "Isageum," Saroguk attacked and conquered neighboring states like Eumjupbeolguk (present-day Angang), Apdokguk (present-day Gyeongsan), and Gammunguk (present-day Gimcheon). These conquests highlight the crucial role of iron production in Saroguk's emergence as the dominant power in Jinhan.

040
Molds

Hwangseong-dong, Gyeongju
Silla, 3rd-4th century CE
L. 22.3 cm (far right)

041
Tuyere

Hwangseong-dong, Gyeongju
Silla, 3rd-4th century CE
L. 42.5 cm

• Gueo-ri Tomb 1

Gueo-ri Tomb 1, which is located atop a hill in Gueo-ri, Oedong-eup, Gyeongju, is a large wooden cist tomb, with a main burial cist where the deceased was laid to rest and an auxiliary cist containing only grave goods. Laid out on the floor of the main burial cist were approximately fifty iron socketed spearheads, forty iron axes, and twenty iron ingots. The auxiliary cist yielded *wajil* pottery and pieces of armor, including a neck guard and waist guard. The presence of highly advanced armor and the arrangement of numerous iron artifacts that appear to be ceremonial, rather than intended for practical use, was likely meant to display the power and military prowess of a Saroguk ruler who had dominated surrounding territories.

042
Gorget and Waist Armor
Gueo-ri Tomb 1, Gyeongju
Silla, 3rd century CE
H. 22.0 cm (gorget)

043
Gueo-ri Tomb 1 Excavated Artifacts
Guero-ri Tomb 1, Gyeongju
Silla, 3rd century CE
H. 36.4 cm (vessel stand)

044
Chamfron

Sara-ri, Gyeongju
Silla, 5th century CE
L. 48.0 cm

A chamfron is a piece of armor for protecting the head of a horse, and consists of the main headplate, visor plate, ear guards, and cheek guards. Among these pieces, the main headplate is particularly important for identifying the lineage and chronology of the armor. Headplates that are divided in the center can be traced back to northeast China, while undivided headplates are believed to have originated in Goguryeo.

045
Plate Armor

Gujeong-dong, Gyeongju
Silla, 4th century CE
H. 71.0 cm (including gorget)

Excavated from Gujeong-dong, Gyeongju, this suit of armor was made by connecting several rectangular iron plates in a vertical arrangement. It also includes a neck guard formed by several rectangular iron plates arranged in the shape of a fan. This is considered to be one of the oldest examples of iron armor ever found in Korea, along with the armor pieces discovered at Jungsan-ri, Ulsan and Sara-ri, Gyeongju.

046
Plate Armor

Dongsan-ri Tomb 34, Gyeongju
Silla, 4th century CE
H. 52.0 cm
(including gorget)

047
Plate Armor

Masan-ri, Pohang
Silla, 4th century CE
H. 69.1 cm
(including gorget)

048
Plate Armor

Sara-ri, Tomb 55, Gyeongju
Silla, 5th century CE
H. 60.5 cm (except helmet)

This type of plate armor, which is formed by joining multiple rectangular plates together side by side, is unique to Korea, having only been found at sites of Silla or Gaya. There are some regional discrepancies between the two, as Silla plate armor features a trumpet-shaped neck guard, while Gaya neck guards are semi-circular in shape. Silla plate armor is generally undecorated, with an emphasis on function over displays of prestige. From the late fourth century onward, Silla plate armor was gradually replaced by lamellar armor, in which numerous smaller scales are laced together, showing the influence of Goguryeo.

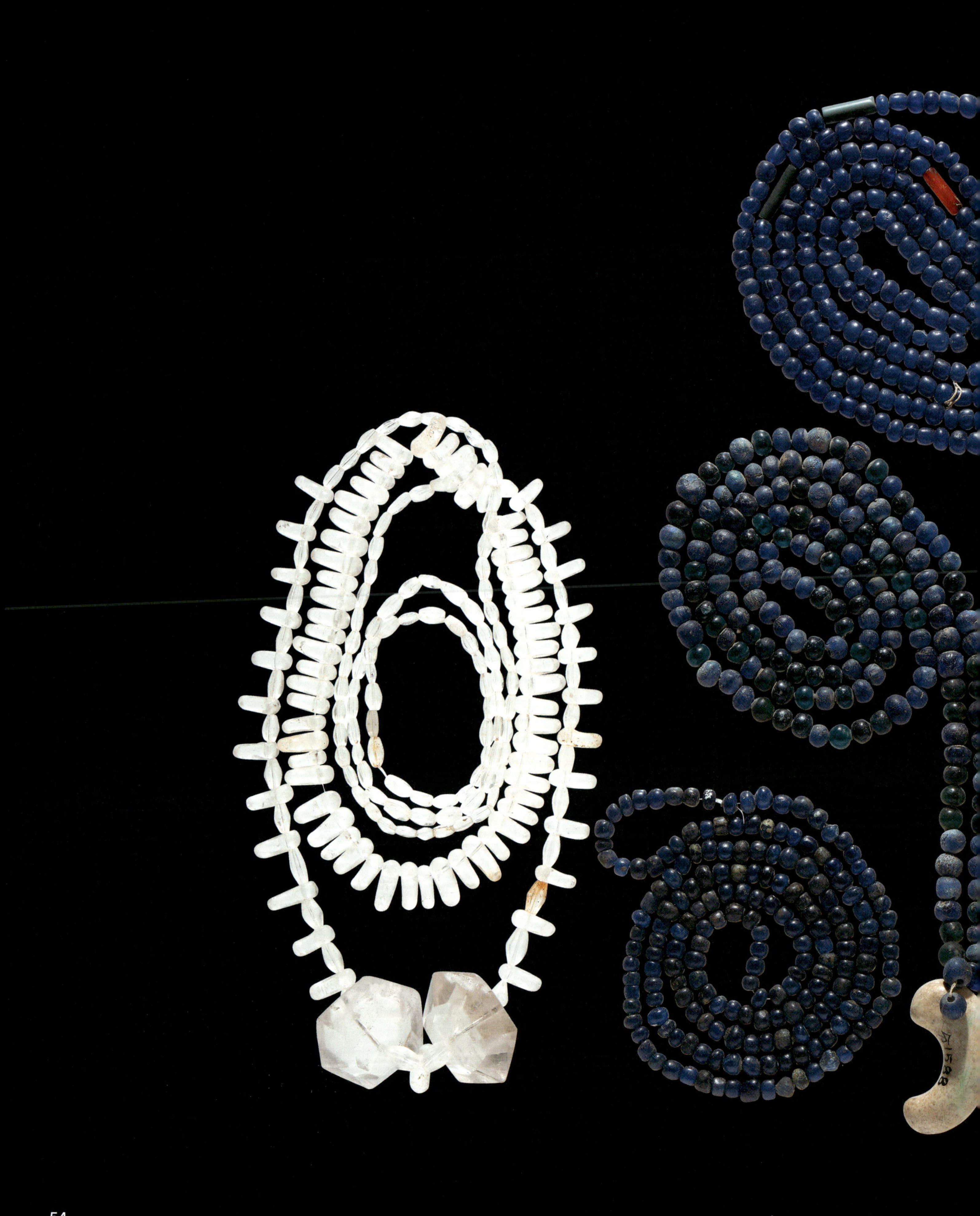

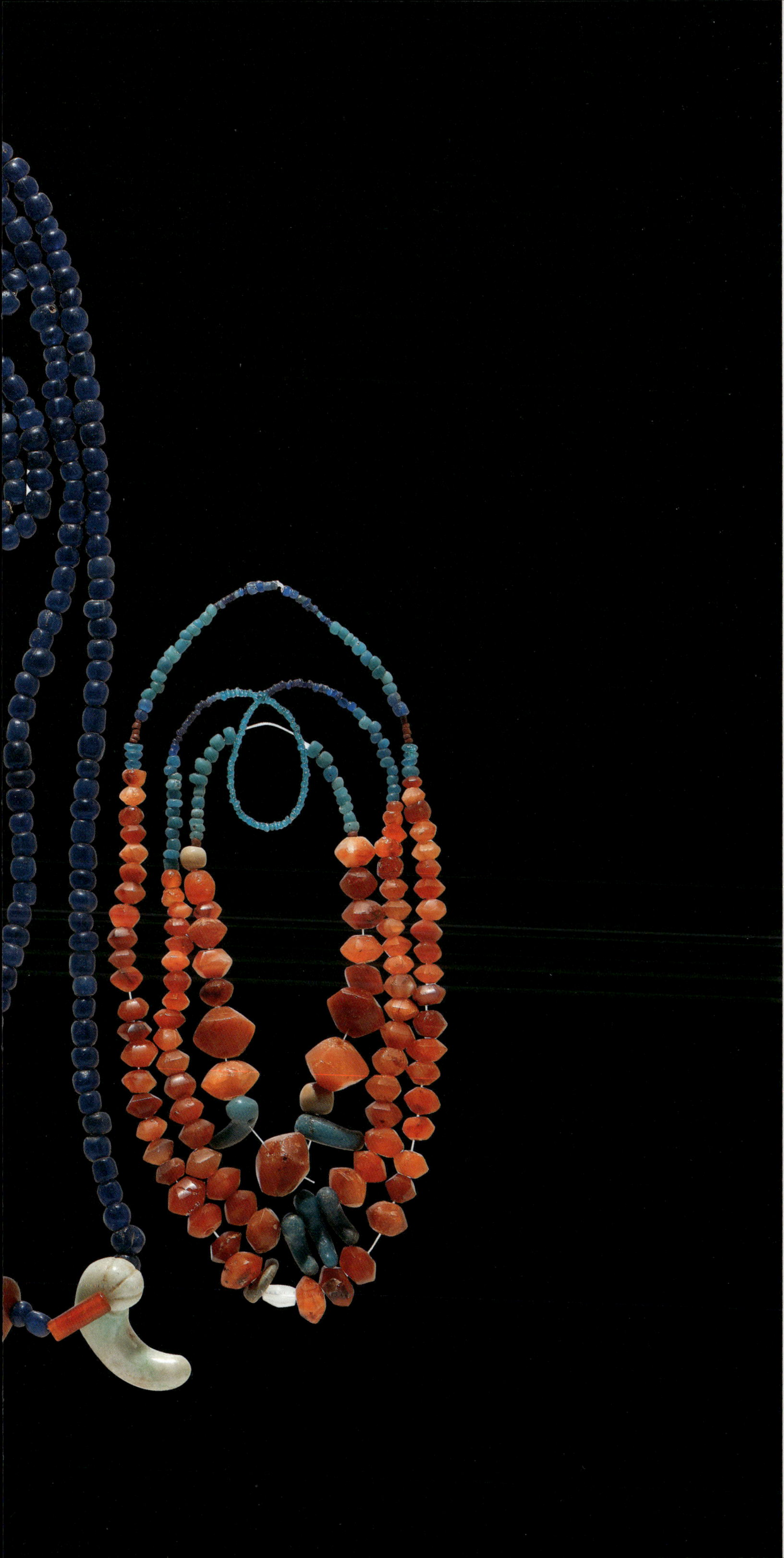

049
Necklaces

Gyeongju
Silla, 3rd century CE
L. 46.5 cm (far left)

In the "Accounts of Han" section of the "Book of Wei" from the "Biography of the Eastern Barbarians" in *Sanguozhi* (*Records of the Three Kingdoms*), written in the third century, it states that, "The people of Samhan regarded beads as treasures, which they used to decorate their clothes and hung from their necks or ears." Supporting this record, an abundance of beads has been excavated from Samhan tombs. At first, blue glass beads were predominant, but over time, a wider variety of beads appeared in bright colors and different materials (primarily crystal, but also agate and glass). The beads are generally classified according to their shape: spherical, curved, or multi-faceted.

III.

Silla's Development and Expansion

 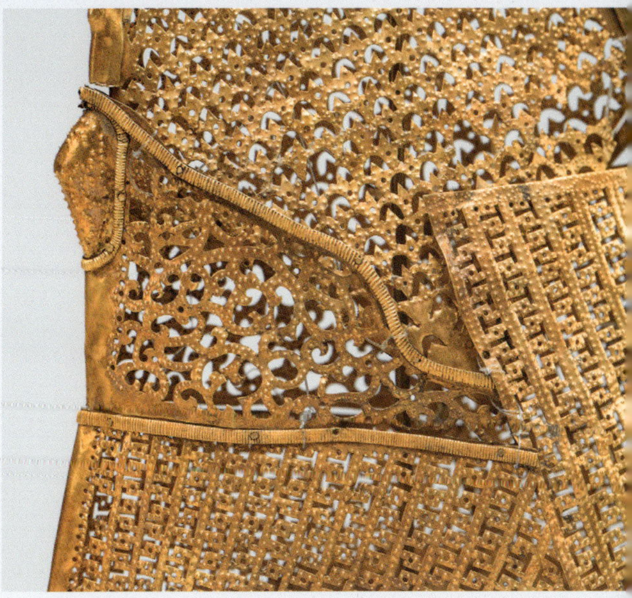

By continually conquering neighboring polities and expanding its territory over time, Saroguk steadily evolved into the new state of Silla. Early on, Silla actively conducted international exchange, but its foreign trade networks were crippled by the collapse of the Nangnang (Lelang) and Daebang (Daifang) Commanderies in the early fourth century CE. In response, the fledgling state of Silla redirected its efforts toward internal consolidation, culminating with its integration of the Jinhan Confederacy in the mid-fourth century. This expansion was accompanied by a transition to a monarchist political structure, as the ruling power of six aristocratic clans was consolidated into a single royal authority with the title of "*Maripgan*," meaning "supreme chief." The first ruler to hold this title was Naemul Maripgan (r. 356–402) of the Kim clan, who enacted a system of hereditary rule and thus established a dynastic monopoly. The "Maripgan" title remained in use until 503, when Jijeung (r. 500–514), formally adopted the Chinese title of "*Wang*," or "king." The emergence of royal power in this period is further evidenced by the construction of monumental wooden chamber tombs with stone mounds, which are still found throughout the Gyeongju basin.

In this early period, Silla maintained diplomatic relations with Goguryeo, which assisted the new kingdom in dispatching envoys to Chinese dynasties. However, these interactions enabled Goguryeo to extend its political influence over Silla. Following the southern campaigns of King Gwanggaeto the Great, the ninth king of Goguryeo (r. 391–412), Silla essentially fell under the power of Goguryeo's hegemony. For example, both Silsung Maripgan (r. 402-417) and Nulji Maripgan (r. 417–458) were held as hostages in Goguryeo as youths, and even after their release, Goguryeo continued to interfere in Silla's royal succession. Nevertheless, beginning with the reign of Nulji Maripgan, Silla gradually extricated itself from Goguryeo's dominion and developed into a fully autonomous state.

The Maripgan and the Peak of Silla's Gold Culture

The peak of Silla's gold culture lasted from the fifth to the early sixth century, a span of about 150 years. In this period, the ruling families of Silla expressed their wealth and status by constructing grand tombs in the heart of the kingdom and lavishly adorning the deceased with crowns and other ornaments of gold. Since gold never tarnishes, it was used to symbolize the eternal power and nobility of the ruler. The gold culture initially flourished in the Silla capital of Gyeongju, as represented by the construction of Hwangnamdaechong Tomb in the fifth century. Around the same time, the gold culture spread to surrounding regions, as local leaders of Gyeongsan, Daegu, Uiseong, Sangju, and Yangsan received gold ornaments symbolizing their acquiescence to the crown. However, the distributed gold ornaments show key differences in material quality and composition, indicating that gold items outside the capital were subject to strict regulations.

After Silla unified the Three Kingdoms in the mid-seventh century, the gold objects that once filled royal tombs were largely replaced by gilt-bronze substitutes, with the notable exception of gold earrings. But this shift did not mark the end of Silla's gold culture, as gold continued to play a prominent role in the society, particularly in the adornment of palaces and Buddhist temples.

050
Gold Bowls
Wolseong-ro Tomb Ga-13, Gyeongju
Silla, 4th-5th century CE
H. 5.2 cm (left)

051
Gold Dangling Pendants
Wolseong-ro Tomb Ga-13, Gyeongju
Silla, 4th-5th century CE
L. 26.4 cm (far right)

052
Gold Ornaments
Wolseong-ro Tomb Ga-13, Gyeongju
Silla, 4th-5th century CE
L. 65.3 cm (far right)

• Silla Gold Crowns

Today, there are six known gold crowns from Silla, which were respectively discovered in Gyo-dong, in the north mound of Hwangnamdaechong Tomb, and in the tombs of Geumgwanchong, Seobongchong, Geumnyeongchong, and Cheonmachong. Such crowns were produced throughout the fifth and sixth centuries and are believed to have been worn by royalty during the Maripgan period. They were made by cutting, shaping, and bending thin sheets of gold, which were then decorated with spangles and curved jade beads. Among the six, the gold crown from Gyo-dong is considered to be the earliest, because the side branches of its upright decorations are angled, as opposed to the perpendicular side branches on later Silla crowns. The other five crowns, including the one from Hwangnamdaechong Tomb, exemplify the quintessential form of Silla gold crowns, with tree-shaped uprights in the center and antler-shaped uprights on both sides, all affixed to a headband. The number of tiers on the tree-shaped uprights seems to have increased over time, as crowns from the late fifth century generally have three tiers, while those from the first half of the sixth century have four tiers.

053
Gold Crown
Gyo-dong, Gyeongju
Silla, 5th century CE
H. 12.8 cm

054
Gold Crown
North Mound of
Hwangnamdaechong Tomb, Gyeongju
Silla, 5th century CE
H. 27.3 cm
National Treasure

055
Gold Crown
Seobongchong Tomb, Gyeongju
Silla, 5th century CE
H. 35.0 cm
Treasure

056
Gold Crown

Geumgwanchong Tomb, Gyeongju
Silla, 5th century CE
H. 27.5 cm
National Treasure

• **Gold Crown from Cheonmachong Tomb**

The most elaborate of the six extant Silla gold crowns is the one from Cheonmachong Tomb, which consists of a headband with three tree-shaped uprights and two antler-shaped uprights. The tree-shaped uprights have four tiers, with a denser arrangement of trunks and branches than the other crowns. For added splendor, the entire crown is extravagantly adorned with curved jade beads and gold spangles. Both the headband and uprights are incised with continuous patterns of dots, waves, and circles. A pair of long dangling pendants hang from the headband, each consisting of a chain and nib-shaped ornaments suspended from a thin ring.

057
Gold Crown
Geumnyeongchong Tomb, Gyeongju
Silla, 6th century CE
H. 27.0 cm
Treasure

058
Gold Crown

Cheonmachong Tomb, Gyeongju
Silla, 6th century CE
H. 32.5 cm
National Treasure

The Great Tombs: Monuments of the Maripgan

Today, Gyeongju is famous for the numerous giant mounds scattered around its city center, which are in fact large wooden chamber tombs with stone mounds that were built as the final resting places for Silla kings, queens, and aristocrats. Excavations at the tombs of Cheonmachong, Hwangnamdaechong, and Geumgwanchong have revealed details of their construction. Each tomb contains a square wooden chamber where the deceased was laid to rest, along with an assortment of grave goods. This chamber was then covered with a stone mound, followed by an earthen layer. These tombs were prominent from the fifth to the first half of the sixth century, when Silla was still laying the foundations of statehood. In this formative period, when the status of the new ruling class needed to be visibly asserted, the tombs served as monumental symbols of the Maripgan. Excavations of these tombs have uncovered rare foreign artifacts and priceless treasures representing Silla's legendary craftsmanship, highlighted by the ornate gold crowns and other gold objects.

The exact origin of wooden chamber tombs with a stone mound is still up for debate, with some experts having claimed that they can be traced to Siberia. More recently, however, they have come to be considered as a unique type of tomb that emerged independently in Silla.

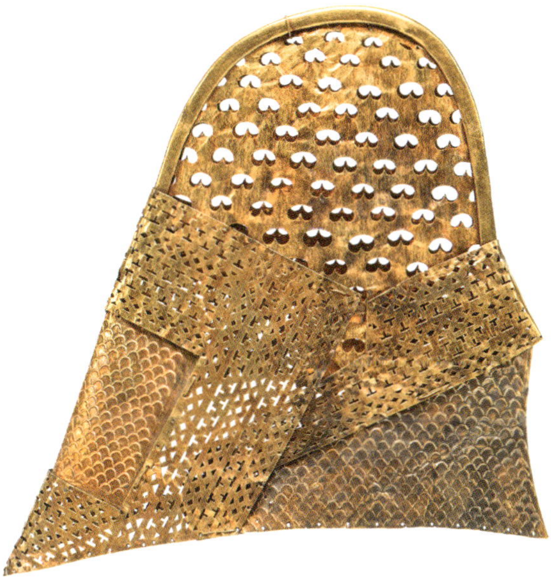

059
Gold Crown Cap
Geumgwanchong Tomb, Gyeongju
Silla, 5th century CE
H. 19.0 cm
National Treasure

• Geumgwanchong Tomb

When it was accidentally discovered in 1921, Geumgwanchong Tomb astonished the world with its unprecedented trove of gold treasures, including a crown, earrings, belt ornaments, bracelets, and rings. As the first tomb with a gold crown ever discovered in Korea, it was named "Geumgwanchong," which literally means, "gold crown tomb." Unfortunately, however, those who unearthed the artifacts were not archaeologists, so there are no detailed records of the original excavation. In 2015, the National Museum of Korea re-excavated the tomb, which revealed that it actually had a double-chamber structure. After the main wooden chamber was erected, stones were stacked against the outer walls, and the entire structure was then sealed with soil.

060
Gold Crown Ornament
Geumgwanchong Tomb, Gyeongju
Silla, 5th century CE
H. 40.8 cm
National Treasure

061
Gold Earrings
Geumgwanchong Tomb, Gyeongju
Silla, 5th century CE
L. 8.7 cm

062
Gold Earrings
Geumgwanchong Tomb, Gyeongju
Silla, 5th century CE
L. 10.0 cm

063
Gold and Silver Ornaments
Geumgwanchong Tomb, Gyeongju
Silla, 5th century CE
L. 14.8 cm
(top right)

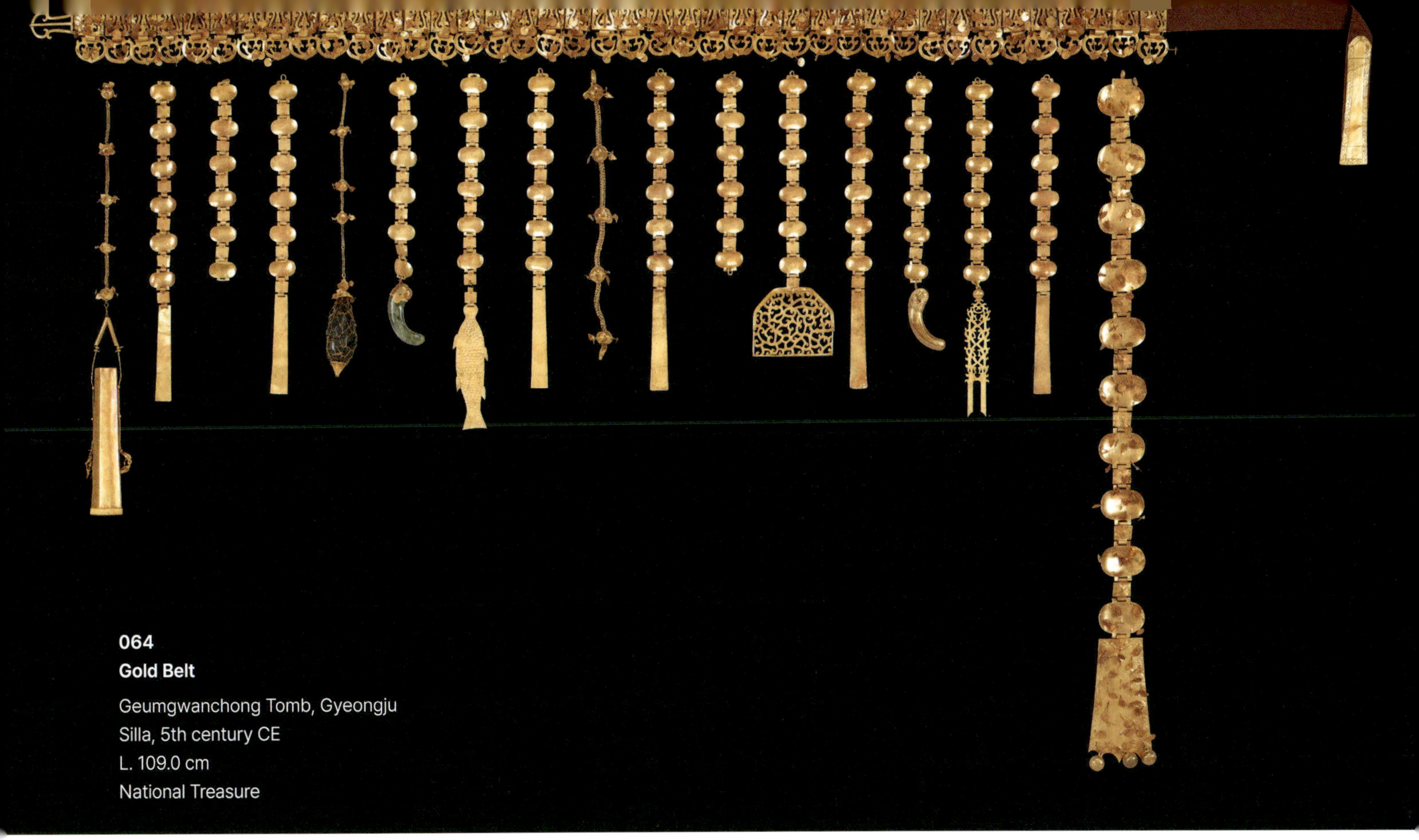

064
Gold Belt

Geumgwanchong Tomb, Gyeongju
Silla, 5th century CE
L. 109.0 cm
National Treasure

065
Large Sword with Ring-shaped Pommel with Inscription: "介斯智王"

Geumgwanchong Tomb, Gyeongju
Silla, 5th century CE
L. 87.0 cm

In 2013, in the process of preserving a large sword excavated from Geumgwanchong Tomb, an inscription was identified at the end of the scabbard, which read "Isajiwang" ("King Isaji"). This was the first time that a king's name had ever been confirmed within a specific Silla tomb. However, there is no record of a Silla king named "Isaji" in any historical documents or epigraphs. Therefore, it is estimated that, at this time, the word "*wang*" was likely used interchangeably with the word "*gan*," which refers to a leader, rather than a king.

Inscription detail

066
Silver Crown Cap

South Mound of Hwangnamdaechong Tomb, Gyeongju
Silla, 5th century CE
H. 15.4 cm

• Hwangnamdaechong Tomb

With a maximum length of 120 meters along its north-south axis and a height of 22 meters, Hwangnamdaechong Tomb is the largest wooden chamber tomb with a stone mound among the Silla royal tombs. It is actually a twin tomb, with two separate tombs placed side by side along the north-south axis. The occupant of the south tomb, which was constructed first, was a male wearing a gilt-bronze crown, while the northern tomb, constructed later, held a female with a gold crown. Based on the scale of the tomb and the exceptional quality of the grave goods, Hwangnamdaechong is strongly believed to be the joint tomb of a Silla king and his queen consort, likely either Naemul Maripgan or Nulji Maripgan.

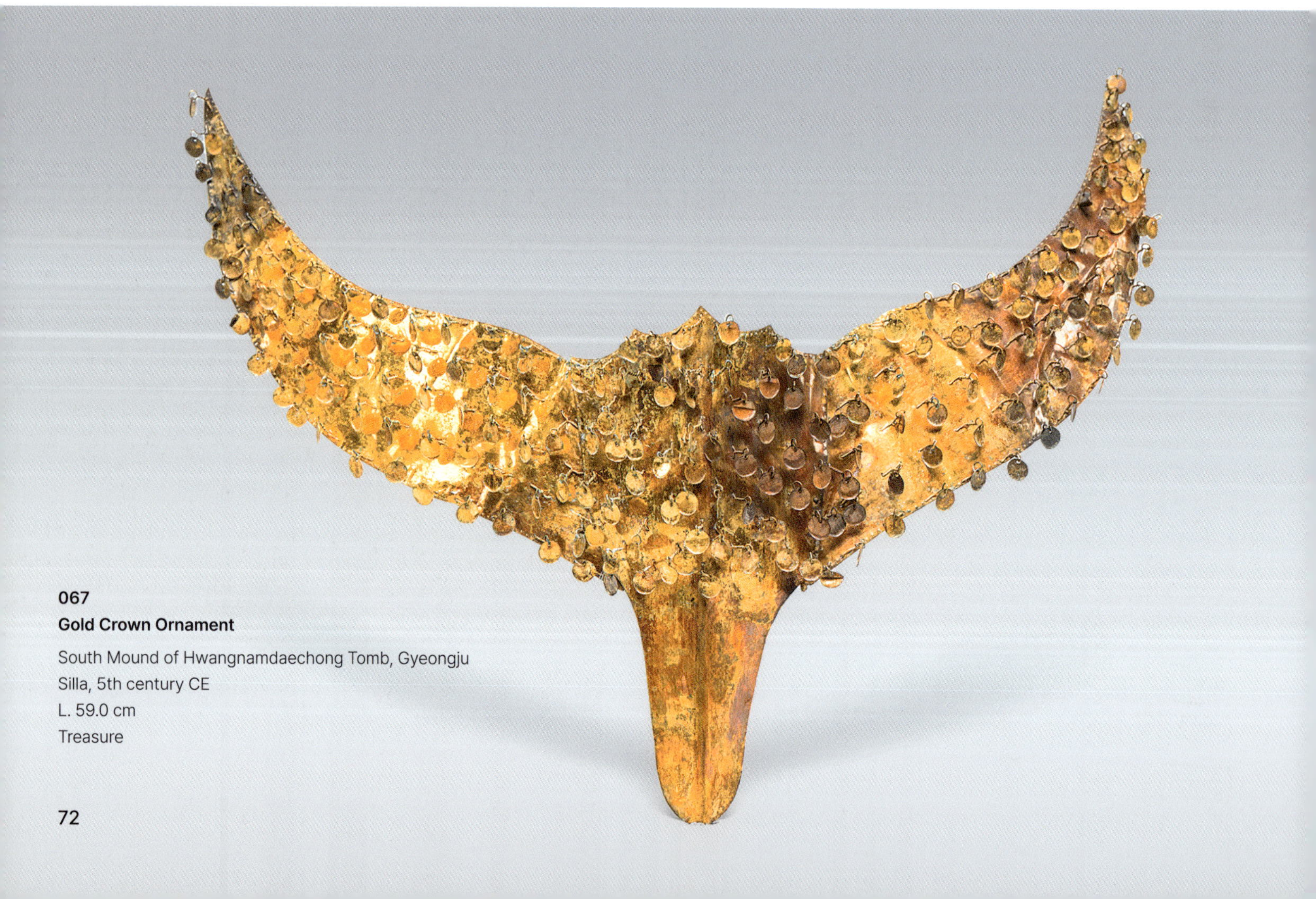

067
Gold Crown Ornament

South Mound of Hwangnamdaechong Tomb, Gyeongju
Silla, 5th century CE
L. 59.0 cm
Treasure

068

Gilt-bronze Belt with Jewel Beetle Wings

South Mound of Hwangnamdaechong Tomb, Gyeongju
Silla, 5th century CE
L. 4.0 cm (each)

Seven segments of this gilt-bronze belt have survived, all of which feature an elaborate openwork dragon design. The back of each section was further adorned with vertical layers of wings from jewel beetles. Containing traces of metallic elements such as iron, copper, and magnesium, the outer wings of jewel beetles have a lustrous red and green sheen. Moreover, the wings of jewel beetles change colors depending on the angle of view. Taking advantage of these traits, Silla craftspeople used the iridescent wings of jewel beetles to decorate gilt-bronze belt ornaments, horse saddle fittings, and stirrups.

Back

Jewel Beetles and Wings

069

Gilt Bronze Shoes

South Mound of Hwangnamdaechong Tomb, Gyeongju
Silla, 5th century CE
L. 34.5 cm

070

Spindle Whorl-shaped Stone Tools

North Mound of Hwangnamdaechong Tomb, Gyeongju
Silla, 5th century CE
D. 8.1 cm

071

Silver Belt

North Mound of Hwangnamdaechong Tomb, Gyeongju

Silla, 5th century CE

L. 51.6 cm

072

Belt-end Section with Inscription: "夫人帶"

North Mound of Hwangnamdaechong Tomb, Gyeongju

Silla, 5th century CE

L. 12.3 cm

Belts made of gold, silver, and bronze were unearthed at Hwangnamdaechong Tomb. Gold ornaments and accessories were reserved exclusively for royalty, who are believed to have worn belts adorned with silver and gilt-bronze decorations as well. Gold and silver belt pieces were discovered in the North Mound of Hwangnamdaechong Tomb, including a silver belt-end section engraved with the characters "夫人帶," meaning "wife's belt," suggesting that the deceased in the north tomb was a woman.

073
Swords with Ring Pommel

South Mound of Hwangnamdaechong Tomb, Gyeongju
Silla, 5th century CE
L. 32.0 cm (far left)

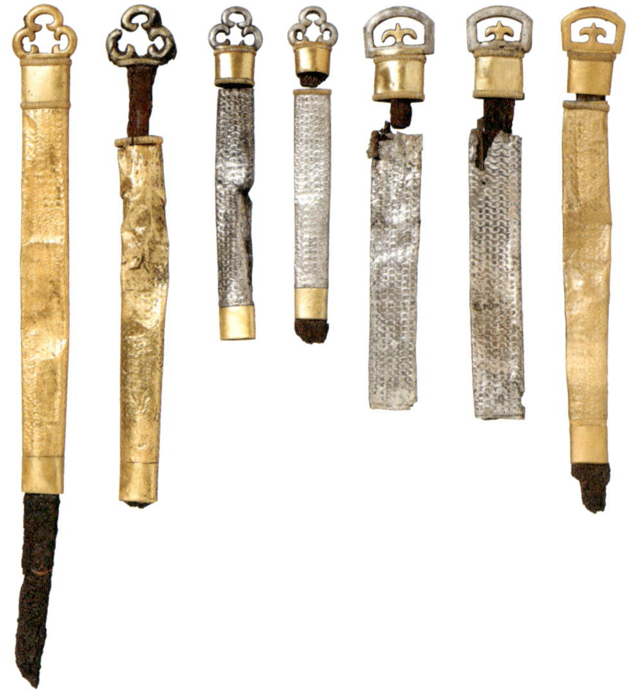

074

Gold and Silver Vessels

Hwangnamdaechong Tomb, Gyeongju
Silla, 5th century CE
H. 9.1. cm (back row, left)

An array of gold and silver vessels has been excavated from the large wooden chamber tombs with stone mounds of Silla, including mounted dishes, covered containers, jars, and bowls. The gold and silver mounted dishes were modeled after earthenware vessels, with the added touch of heart-shaped spangles attached to the rim with gold thread. Notably, the covered containers have a flat bottom and a round knob atop a lotus-shaped lid, details that are not found in Silla pottery. All of these precious metal vessels have been recovered from large royal tombs, indicating that they were produced exclusively for Silla royalty.

075
Bronze Bowls with Lid

South Mound of Hwangnamdaechong Tomb, Gyeongju
Silla, 5th century CE
H. 12.0 cm (far right)

076
Bronze Cauldrons

Hwangnamdaechong Tomb, Gyeongju
Silla, 5th century CE
H. 16.8 cm (right)

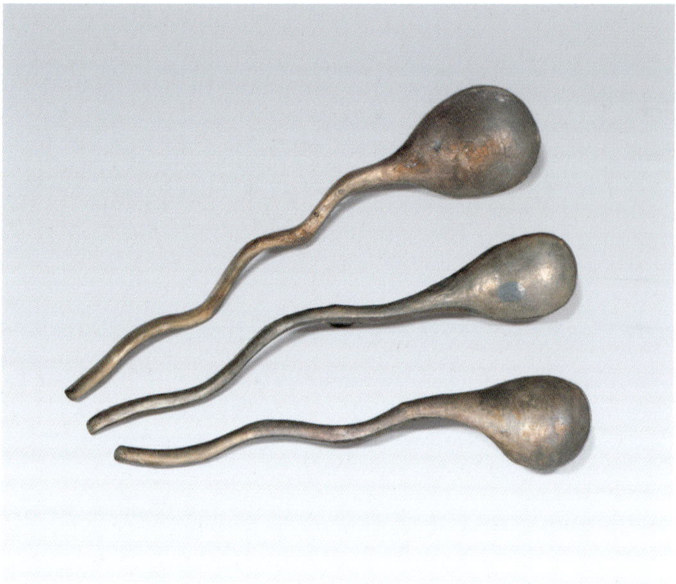

077
Jars with Spout
South Mound of Hwangnamdaechong Tomb, Gyeongju
Silla, 5th century CE
L. 16.2 cm (right)

078
Ladles
South Mound of Hwangnamdaechong Tomb, Gyeongju
Silla, 5th century CE
L. 38.6 cm (top)

079
Gilt-bronze Saddlebow
South Mound of Hwangnamdaechong Tomb, Gyeongju
Silla, 5th century CE
L. 55.3 cm

080
Forearm Covers
South Mound of Hwangnamdaechong Tomb, Gyeongju
Silla, 5th century CE
H. 34.4 cm (front)

081
Stirrups

South Mound of
Hwangnamdaechong Tomb,
Gyeongju
Silla, 5th century CE
L. 23.0 cm (top right)

082
Harness Fittings

South Mound of
Hwangnamdaechong Tomb,
Gyeongju
Silla, 5th century CE
L. 4.8 cm (left)

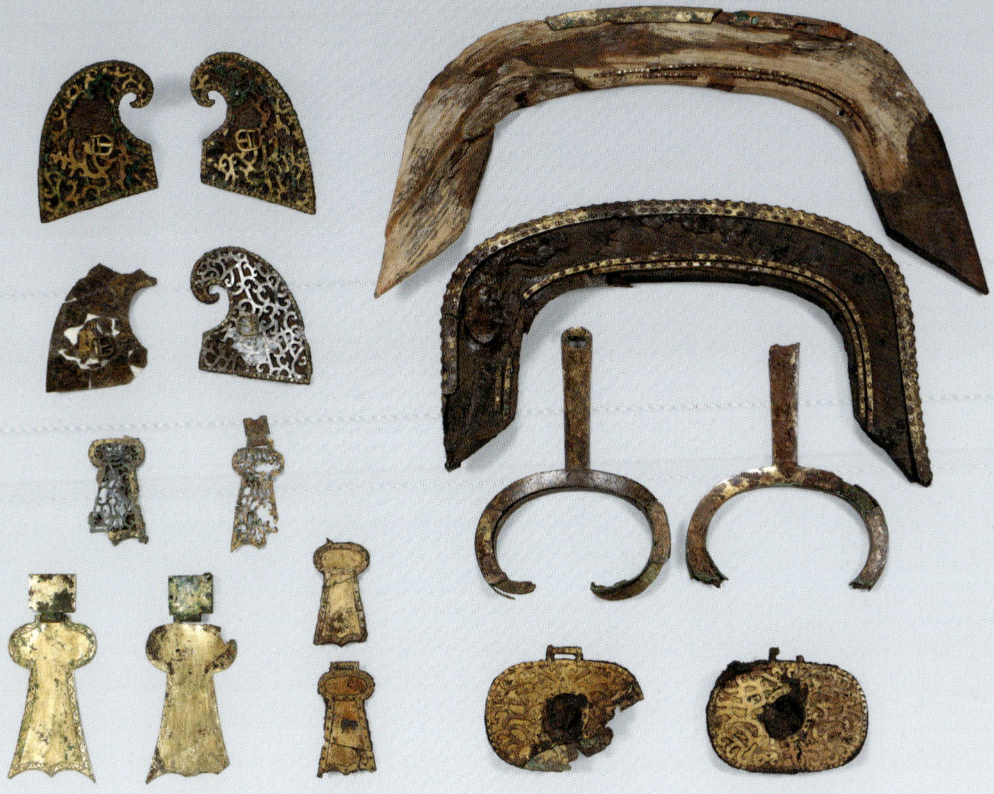

083
Horse Trappings
South Mound of Hwangnamdaechong Tomb, Gyeongju
Silla, 5th century CE
L. 54.7 cm (top left)

084
Horse Trappings
South Mound of Hwangnamdaechong Tomb, Gyeongju
Silla, 5th century CE
L. 13.8 cm (bottom left)

085
Iron Halberds

South Mound of Hwangnamdaechong Tomb, Gyeongju
Silla, 5th century CE
L. 62.2 cm (center)

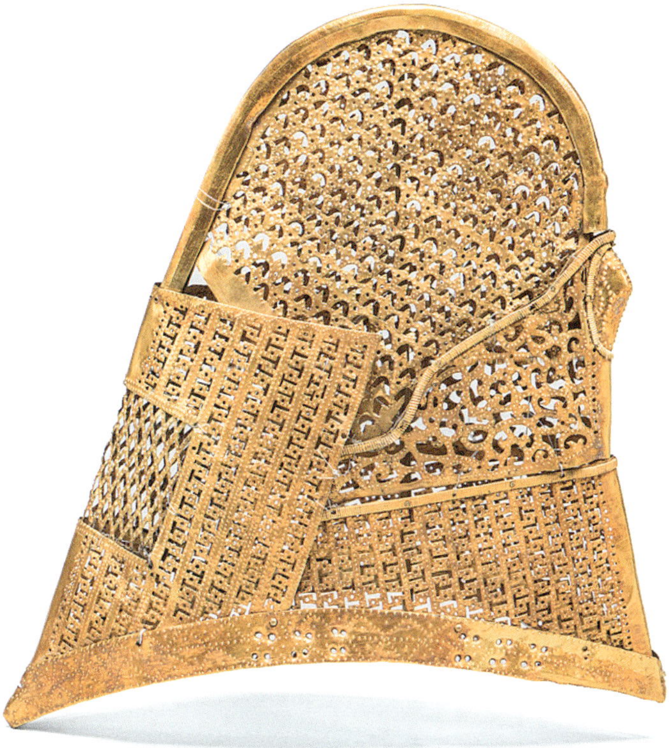

• Cheonmachong Tomb

Cheonmachong Tomb is a medium-sized wooden chamber tomb with a stone mound in the Daereungwon Ancient Tomb Complex in Gyeongju, measuring 47 meters in diameter and 13 meters in height. A separate compartment for grave goods was constructed above the head of the deceased, where various artifacts were discovered, including equipment and accessories for horse-riding. Among these accessories was a pair of saddle flaps bearing the image of the "Cheonma," or "Heavenly Horse." The occupant of the tomb was adorned with a gold crown, gold earrings, a chestlace, a gold belt, and a large sword. The exceptional quality of the gold jewelry and other grave goods suggests that the deceased was a member of royalty or a high-ranking aristocrat from the first half of the sixth century.

086
Gold Crown Cap

Cheonmachong Tomb, Gyeongju
Silla, 6th century CE
H. 19.0 cm
National Treasure

087
Gold Crown Ornament

Cheonmachong Tomb, Gyeongju
Silla, 6th century CE
H. 40.8 cm
Treasure

088
Gold Crown Ornament

Cheonmachong Tomb, Gyeongju
Silla, 6th century CE
H. 23.0 cm
Treasure

089

Bamboo Mudguard with Celestial Horse Painting and Gilt Bronze Ornament

Cheonmachong Tomb, Gyeongju
Silla, 6th century CE
56.0 × 81.0 cm

Saddle flaps are a type of horse tack, which are attached to a saddle to prevent the rider from getting splashed with mud. They come in pairs and are hung from both sides of the saddle. Three different types of saddle flaps were found in the grave goods compartment in Cheonmachong Tomb. The uppermost flaps were made from bamboo, followed by a pair made from birch bark (one placed atop the other), with lacquerware flaps at the bottom. The birch bark saddle flaps are rectangular in shape and feature a painting of a white celestial horse surrounded by a pattern of vines and flowers.

090
Birch Bark Mudguard with Celestial Horse Painting (placed above)

Cheonmachong Tomb, Gyeongju
Silla, 6th century CE
54.7×73.5 cm
National Treasure

091
Birch Bark Mudguard with Celestial Horse Painting (placed below)

Cheonmachong Tomb, Gyeongju
Silla, 6th century CE
55.2×73.2 cm
National Treasure

Golden Objects and Divine Power

During the Maripgan phase of Silla, members of the ruling class displayed their power by wearing clothing and accessories adorned with gold, silver, and bronze. For example, gold crowns and gold belts symbolizing the sanctity and legitimacy of power were used to convey the authority of the supreme ruler. Meanwhile, other elite residents of the Silla capital and leaders of the regional provinces wore gilt-bronze crowns and belts made of either silver or bronze. Those with high status also flaunted their wealth and influence with earrings, pendants, rings, and bracelets lavishly crafted in gold. In addition to gold, the Silla people also adorned themselves with glass and jade beads. Numerous necklaces and chestlaces composed of jade and glass beads have been unearthed from Silla tombs, including Hwangnamdaechong Tomb. Glass, which can be easily shaped and colored, was produced in a wide range of hues, including indigo, white, blue, yellow, green, and red. Inlay techniques were also used to create beads of multiple colors.

092
Gold Ornament
Geumgwanchong Tomb, Gyeongju
Silla, 5th century CE
L. 11.3 cm (triangle)

093
Gold Ornament
Geumgwanchong Tomb, Gyeongju
Silla, 5th century CE
L. 30.0 cm

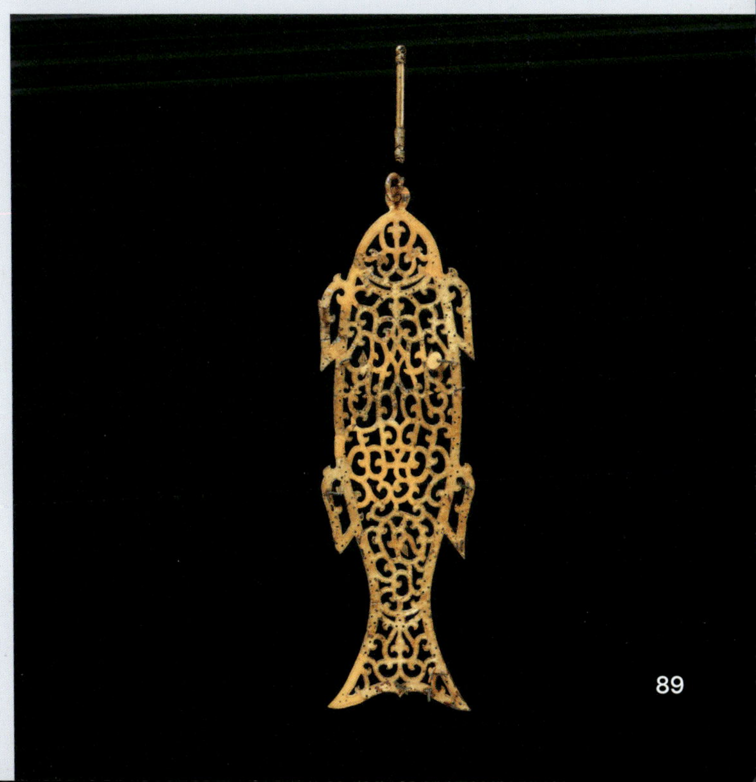

The most common type of personal accessory worn by members of the Silla upper class was earrings. While some Silla earrings consist solely of a simple ring, those found in royal tombs, particularly dating from the sixth century, are amazingly elaborate and ornate, with tiny gold granules attached with advanced soldering and filigree techniques. Other earrings are inlaid with multicolored pieces of jade or glass, showcasing the sophisticated aesthetics and craftsmanship of the Silla people. Silla earrings generally fall into two categories, depending on the thickness of the central ring, with "thick" types thought to have been worn by women and "thin" types by men.

094
Gold Earrings

Hwango-dong Tomb 5, Gyeongju
Silla, 5th-6th century CE
L. 8.5 cm

095
Gold Earrings

Cheonmachong Tomb, Gyeongju
Silla, 6th century CE
L. 6.0 cm

096
Gold Earrings

Cheonmachong Tomb, Gyeongju
Silla, 6th century CE
L. 5.0 cm

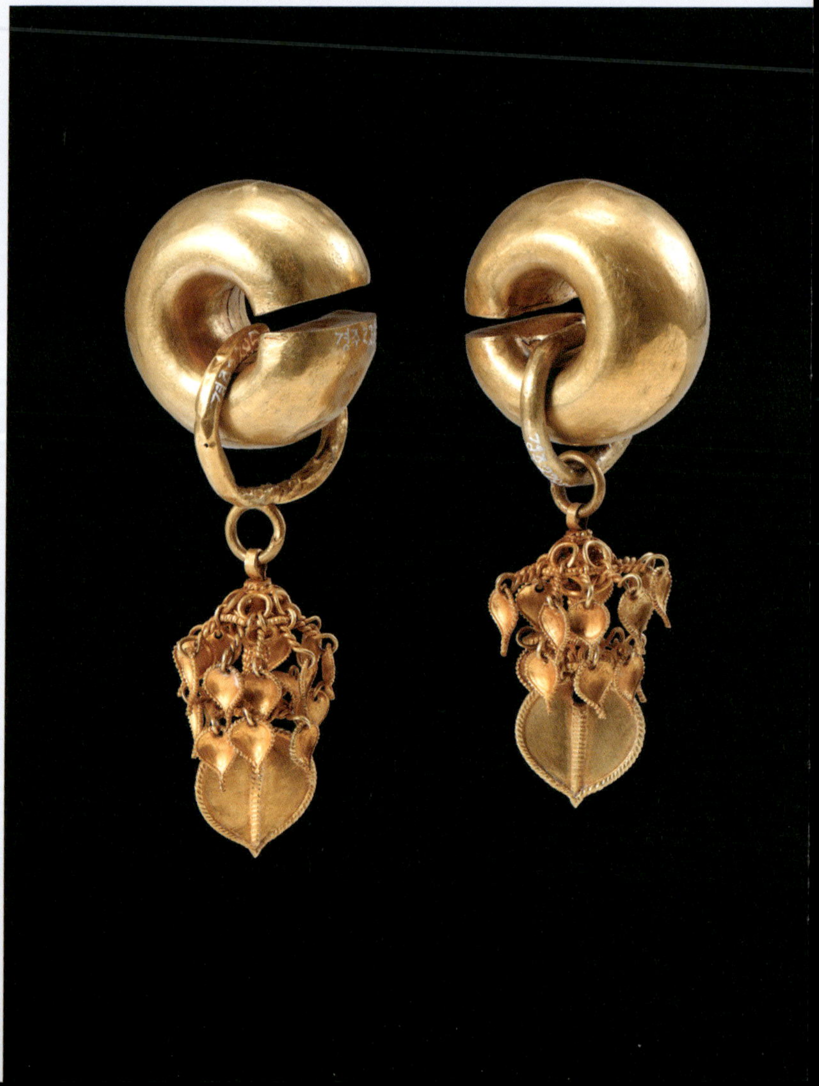

097
Gold Earrings
Hwango-dong Tomb 4, Gyeongju
Silla, 5th-6th century CE
L. 9.6 cm

098
Gold Earrings
Cheonmachong Tomb, Gyeongju
Silla, 6th century CE
L. 6.2 cm

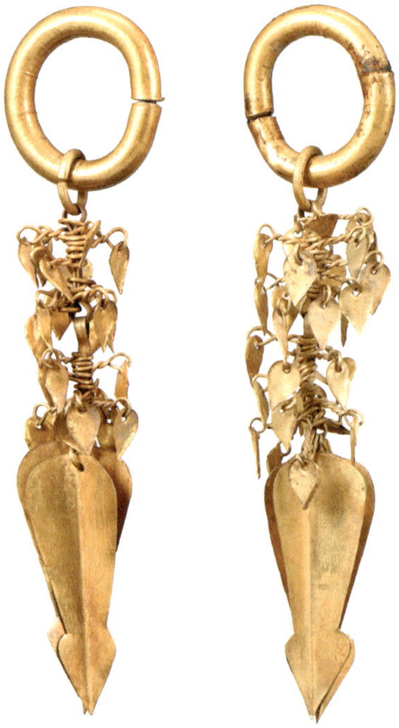

099
Gold Earrings
Noseo-dong Tomb 138, Gyeongju
Silla, 5th-6th century CE
L. 10.5 cm

100
Gold Earrings
Gyerim-ro Tomb 14, Gyeongju
Silla, 5th-6th century CE
L. 7.0 cm

101
Gold Earrings
South Mound of Hwangnamdaechong Tomb, Gyeongju
Silla, 5th century CE
L. 5.5 cm

102
Gold Earrings
Hwango-dong Tomb 14, Gyeongju
Silla, 5th century CE
L. 6.1 cm

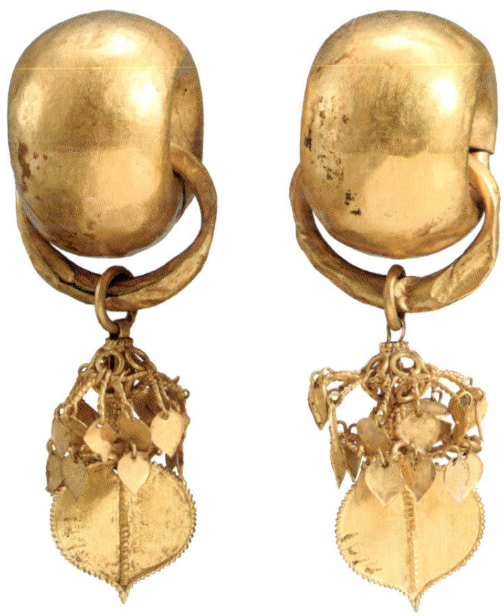

103
Gold Earrings
Hwangnam-dong Tomb 151, Gyeongju
Silla, 5th-6th century CE
L. 7.3 cm

104
Gold Earrings
Hwangnam-dong Tomb 82, Gyeongju
Silla, 5th-6th century CE
L. 6.9 cm

105
Gold Dangling Pendants

North Mound of Hwangnamdaechong Tomb, Gyeongju
Silla, 5th century CE
L. 19.2 cm

Silla gold crowns were often adorned with dangling pendants of various shapes, which hung down from the headband. These pendants typically consist of an upper ring holding a long chain of identical connected ornaments, with a larger central pendant at the bottom. The long chain of connected ornaments often has spangles tightly attached with gold thread and either a nib-shaped gold piece or curved jade at the end. In some cases, pairs of such pendants have been found in tombs with no accompanying crown, but they are still generally assumed to have been crown decorations.

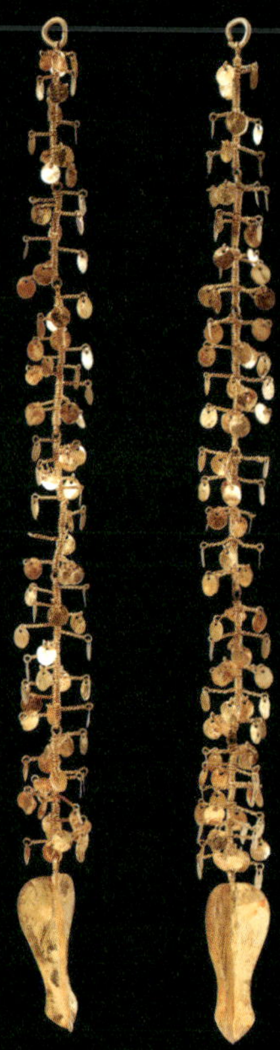

106
Gold Dangling Pendants

North Mound of Hwangnamdaechong Tomb, Gyeongju
Silla, 5th century CE
L. 25.9 cm

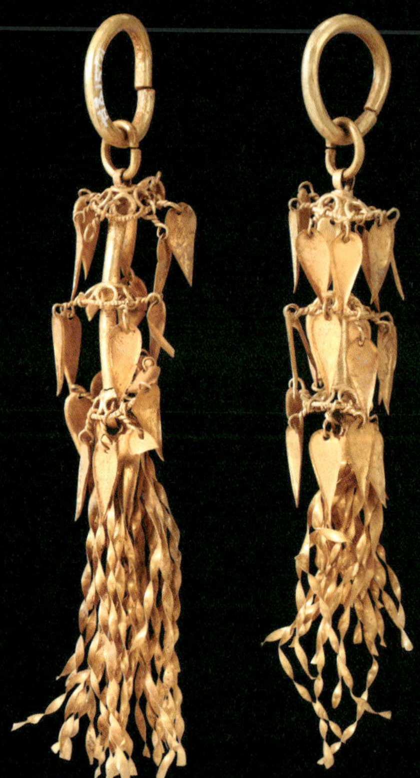

107
Gold Dangling Pendants

Hwango-dong, Gyeongju
Silla, 5th-6th century CE
L. 9.0 cm

108

Gold Dangling Pendants

Tomb 4 of Michuwangneung Tomb District C, Gyeongju
Silla, 6th century CE
L. 16.8 cm
Treasure

109
Gold Dangling Pendants
Gyo-dong, Gyeongju
Silla, 5th century CE
L. 13.0 cm

110
Gold Dangling Pendants
North Mound of Hwangnamdaechong Tomb, Gyeongju
Silla, 5th century CE
L. 18.5 cm

111
Gold Dangling Pendants
Hwango-dong, Gyeongju
Silla, 5th-6th century CE
L. 20.6 cm

112

Gold and Silver Rings

Gyeongju
Silla, 5th-6th century CE
D. 2.5 cm (bottom row, center)

A variety of gold and silver rings with different designs have been unearthed in Silla tombs. They are usually found on the fingers of the deceased, although some have also been discovered on top of the compartment for grave goods or on the burial chamber itself. The rings typify the quintessential aesthetics of Silla, combining both splendor and simplicity. For example, the rings from Cheonmachong Tomb have a simple design with points extending up and down in the middle.

113

Gold Bracelets

Indongchong Tomb, Gyeongju · Cheonmachong Tomb, Gyeongju · North Mound of Hwangnamdaechong Tomb, Gyeongju
Silla, 5th-6th century CE
D. 7.3 cm (far left)

Silla bracelets were primarily made of gold, silver, or gilt-bronze. Most were formed by bending solid rods of gold or silver, although some are hollow. Bracelets from the fifth century are either unadorned, such as the one from the north mound of Hwangnam daechong Tomb, or decorated with a simple notched pattern, as seen in the example from Geumgwanchong Tomb. By the sixth century, bracelets with rounded bumps became popular, as demonstrated by those from Cheonmachong Tomb. Bracelets decorated with glass, dragon motifs, or inlays of bright blue turquoise have also been found in Silla royal tombs.

Detail

114

Gold Necklace

South Mound of Hwangnamdaechong Tomb, Gyeongju
Silla, 5th century CE
L. 66.4 cm
National Treasure

115
Chestlace

Wolseong-ro Tomb Ga-13, Gyeongju
Silla, 4th-5th century CE
L. 43.5 cm

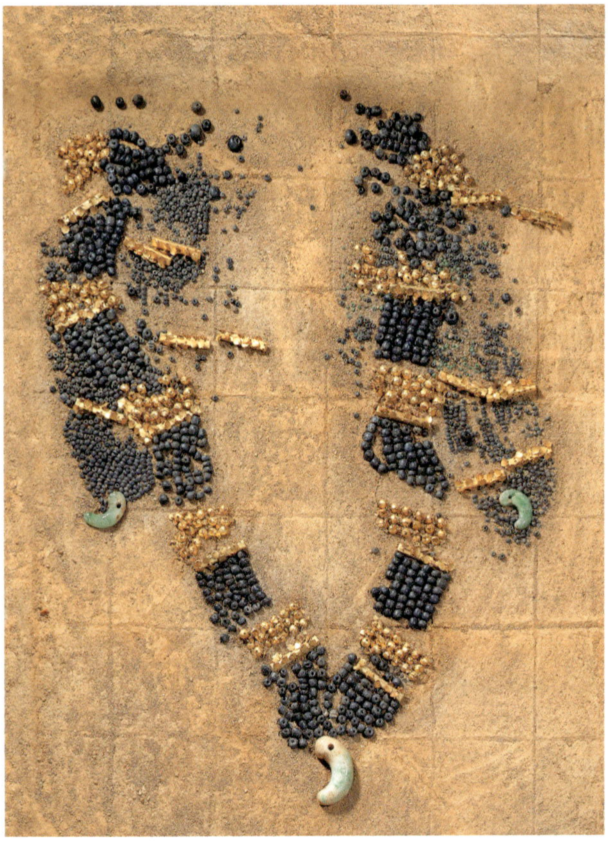

116
Chestlace

Cheonmachong Tomb, Gyeongju
Silla, 6th century CE
L. 63.0 cm
Treasure

Unlike a regular necklace worn around the neck, a chestlace is draped across the shoulders and chest, sometimes hanging down over the stomach. The chestlace from Cheonmachong Tomb is composed of six rows of blue and light green glass beads, interspersed with gold beads. When worn, it would have formed a "U" shape across the chest, with the two upper ends extending over the back. A single large, curved jade piece was attached at the bottom of the chestlace, with smaller jade pieces on either side. Six gold plates were attached at intervals to prevent the strings of beads from tangling, while also enhancing the overall decorative effect.

Production and Spread of Silla Pottery

Excavations of Silla sites have yielded both hard and soft pottery vessels, which are grayish-blue in color. The hard pottery of Silla was shaped on a potter's wheel and fired in enclosed kilns at high temperatures exceeding 1,000°C, resulting in very hard surfaces that make a metallic sound when tapped. They include both everyday vessels, such as jars, mounted dishes, cups with handles, lidded bowls, and vessel stands, and figurative pottery vessels shaped like animals, boats, carts, and lanterns. They also show a wide variety of decorative patterns and designs. Early examples of jars may feature patterns of waves or dots on the neck, shoulder, or lid. Over time, geometric patterns of lines, circles, triangles, and saw-tooth motifs became more common. As the demand for grave goods increased, Silla pottery began to be mass-produced, and thus more standardized. From the fifth century onward, as Silla extended its territory and influence, standardized Silla pottery also spread into the newly incorporated areas. While the pottery found within Silla territory generally shows a consistent style, slight regional variations have been observed.

117
Various Types of Pottery

South Mound of Hwangnamdaechong Tomb,
Gyeongju · Goesi-ri, Yeongdeok
Silla, 5th-6th century CE
H. 10.5 cm (far left)

118
Vessel Stands and Mounted Long-necked Jars

Deokcheon-ri, Gyeongju · Inwang-dong, Gyeongju ·
South Mound of Hwangnamdaechong Tomb, Gyeongju · Goesi-ri, Yongdok
Silla, 5th-6th century CE
H. 43.9 cm (far left)

119

Vessel Stand and Mounted Dishes with Lid

North Mound of Hwangnamdaechong Tomb, Gyeongju
Silla, 5th century CE
H. 16.4 cm (vessel stand)

120

Vessel Stands

South Mound of Hwangnamdaechong Tomb, Gyeongju
Silla, 5th century CE
H. 53.8 cm (back)

121

Figurative Pottery

Deokcheon-ri, Gyeongju · Sara-ri, Gyeongju · Michuwangneung Tomb District, Gyeongju
Silla, 4th-6th century CE
H. 20.0 cm (far left)

122
House-shaped Pottery

Sara-ri, Gyeongju
Silla, 4th century CE
H. 20.3 cm

This unique pottery vessel is shaped like a house set atop a tall mount. The house has a plain gabled roof with no ridges, likely representing a thatched roof. It also displays various architectural details from the period, such as the supporting beams beneath the roof, windows with handles, and the round hole on one side of the roof, which seems to represent a chimney. These types of shaped pottery vessels are believed to have been placed in burials with the hope that the deceased would enjoy the same comforts in the afterlife as they did in life.

123
Auspicious Animal-shaped Pottery

Tomb 3 of Michuwangneung Tomb District C, Gyeongju
Silla, 6th century CE
H. 12.5 cm
Treasure

This auspicious animal has a distinctive appearance, with the round, flat body of a turtle and the head and tail of a dragon. The facial features are depicted in great detail, including the bulging eyes, long tongue, and gaping mouth that appears ready to erupt with flames. The divine appearance is enhanced by twelve dorsal fins running from the head to the tail. A hemispheric funnel rises from the creature's back, and a cylindrical spout extends at an angle from the lower neck. Six dangling ornaments resembling earrings are attached around the edge of the body.

In Korea, ancient clay figurines of people or animals are called "*tou.*" Silla *tou* figurines have primarily been found in and around the central tombs of Gyeongju, including Nodong-dong Tomb 11, Tomb B6 in Jjoksaem, the tombs at the Hwangnam-dong site, and near the Tomb of King Michu. Human *tou* figurines are typically rendered in a simple and playful manner, reflecting the lifestyle of the time, and are generally associated with shamanist prayers or rituals for fertility and abundance. Animal *tou* figurines also tend to be rather succinct, though surprisingly realistic in depiction. The earliest Silla *tou* figurines were attached to the lids of mounted dishes or long-necked jars, which were likely placed in tombs as grave goods.

124
Human · Animal Clay Figurines

Hwangnam-dong, Gyeongju · Provenance Unknown
Silla, 5th-6th century CE
H. 26.0 cm (back row, left)

125

Pottery with Clay Figurines

Wolseong-ro Tomb, Gyeongju · Provenance Unknown
Silla, 5th-6th century CE
H. 11.0 cm (left)

126
Lid with Images

Gyerim-ro Tomb 47, Gyeongju
Silla, 5th century CE
D. 15.0 cm

127
Lid with Horse Images

Provenance Unknown
Silla, 5th-6th century CE
D. 21.0 cm

128
Jar with Clay Figurines

Michuwangneung Tomb District 12, Gyeongju
Silla, 5th century CE
H. 40.5 cm
National Treasure

This jar was excavated in 1973 near the Tomb of King Michu, by the Daereungwon Ancient Tomb Complex in Gyeongju. It is decorated with a number of lively *tou* figurines, including three separate depictions of a snake biting the hind leg of a frog or duck, arranged at regular intervals around the neck and shoulder. The figures between the snakes include a man with enlarged genitals, a man playing a Silla-style *gayageum* (stringed instrument resembling a zither), and other men and women in sexual positions, along with various fish, birds, and turtles. The male figure with the enlarged phallus is missing other body parts, including the head, and the female figures are larger than the men, seemingly emphasizing women as representations of fertility. The delightful vibrancy of the depictions and the coarseness of the clay enable these *tou* figurines to express the daily lives and overall mindset of the Silla people.

IV.

Unification of the Three Kingdoms and Silla's Prosperity

In 503, Jijeung Maripgan officially named his country "Silla," meaning "virtue is renewed each day and spreads in the four directions." He also changed his title as the ruler from "*Maripgan*" to the Chinese royal title "*Wang*," before then establishing new administrative units for provinces and counties in 505. In 520, King Beopheung (r. 514–540) enacted various codes and regulations, including the "bone-rank" system and official rank system, and made Buddhism the state religion. King Jinheung (r. 540–576) expanded Silla's territory through active wars of conquest, and advanced into the Han River region in 551, establishing a crucial bridgehead for foreign trade. King Muyeol (r. 654–661) actively engaged in military diplomacy and adopted cultural elements and institutions from China's Tang Dynasty, creating an alliance that enabled Silla to conquer Baekje in 660. In 668, under King Munmu, the allied Silla-Tang army besieged Pyongyang, the capital of Goguryeo, and forced the surrender of King Bojang. Having thus unified the Three Kingdoms of Korea, Silla then embarked on a new war with its former ally the Tang Dynasty, which had revealed its ambition to take over Silla. Silla won its war with the Tang, thanks to major victories in the Battle of Maesoseong (present-day Yeoncheon, Gyeonggi-do Province) in 675 and the Battle of Gibeolpo (present-day Seocheon, Chungcheongnam-do Province) in 676.

Success in these wars of unification increased the power and authority of the Silla royal court, which was further strengthened by the political system and Confucianist tenets adopted from the Tang Dynasty. The role and authority of the Hwabaek council of high-ranking aristocrats, led by the Sangdaedeung, steadily diminished in conjunction with the rising power of the king's own administrative office, the Jipsabu (state secretariat), and its head, the Jungsi (chief minister). The capital city and regional areas were reorganized into an administrative system of nine provinces and five regional capitals, and a military system of nine *seodang* and ten *jeong*. To further subdue the aristocratic class that posed the greatest possible threat to the throne, the system of *nokeup*, which enabled landowners to collect taxes from locals, was abolished, and salaries were dispersed by the central government according to rank. Through all of these measures, the power of the Silla royalty was continuously strengthened.

Acceptance of Buddhism and Strengthening of Royal Power

Buddhism is said to have been transmitted to Silla by Mukhoja, a monk from Goguryeo, during the reign of Nulji Maripgan (r. 417–458). At the time, Silla did not have a representative state religion, and aristocrats and other citizens worshipped their own ancestor gods or the gods of local mountains and streams. Due to opposition from aristocrats and conflicts with traditional beliefs, Buddhism was not fully established in Silla until after the martyrdom of the monk Ichadon in 527 (or 528), around 100 years after its introduction.

Buddhism is characterized by a systematic set of beliefs based on the teachings of Shakyamuni, along with the use of tangible objects of worship. It also strongly promotes the idea of reincarnation, which helped to reconcile social conflicts and provide an ideological basis for a hierarchical order. By emphasizing faith in the Buddha to members of all social classes, the Silla royal court fostered ideological unity while simultaneously deifying the king and other royals. With the earnest support and protection of the royal family, Buddhism eventually developed into the state religion of Silla. The predominance of Buddhism was confirmed in 534 when King Beopheung cleared Cheonkyungrim Forest, which had been considered sacred by the people of Seorabeol (Gyeongju), in order to build Heungnyunsa, Silla's first Buddhist temple.

Strengthening the Ruling System and Fostering the Hwarang

After the sixth century, Silla further strengthened its ruling system by establishing a centralized government, a process that is described in numerous stelae from that period. Valuable information about Silla's political and social reorganization, including new laws, the role of the king, and the mobilization of the people, can be deduced from contemporaneous stelae from Jungseong-ri and Naengsu-ri in Pohang, from Bongpyeong-ri in Uljin, and from the Cheongje Reservoir in Yeongcheon, as well as from the Ojakbi Stele in Daegu (which bears the inscribed date of the "*musul*" year). This strengthening of the governance system helped Silla to significantly expand its territory during the sixth century.
To efficiently manage the expanding territory and train new talent, King Jinheung created the Hwarang organization. Young aristocrats of the *jingol* rank (i.e., "true bone" in the bone-rank system) were anointed as "Hwarang," each of whom was given charge over hundreds or even thousands of followers called "Nangdo." These youth groups traveled to scenic spots to train their minds and bodies, and diligently studied Confucianism and other relevant subjects. The Hwarang organization played a key role in Silla's unification of the Three Kingdoms.

129
Oath Stone Inscribed in the "*Imshin*" Year

Geumjang-ri, Gyeongju
Silla, 6th-7th century CE
H. 32.0 cm
Treasure

This stele records that, on the sixteenth day of the sixth month of the "*imshin*" year, two people vowed to study Confucian ideas and morals for three years, to put these principles into practice, and to actively work for the kingdom if it should become unstable. This inscription confirms that Confucianism had been widely accepted in Silla by that time. "*Imshin*" is a year in the sixty-year Asian calendar cycle, and thus could correspond to various years from the Roman calendar, including 552 (thirteenth year of King Jinheung), 612 (thirty-fourth year of King Jinpyeong), 672 (twelfth year of King Munmu), or 732 (thirty-first year of King Seongdeok). However, based on the sentence structure of the inscription, the stele is believed to have been made before the unification of the Three Kingdoms in 668.

130
Jungseong-ri Stele from Pohang

Jungseong-ri, Pohang
Silla, 501 CE
H. 105.6 cm
National Treasure
Gyeongju National Research Institute of Cultural Heritage

Believed to have been erected in 501, this is the earliest Silla stele yet discovered. The inscription states that individuals named Saganjigung and Ilbujigung had taken the property of Modanbul and were ordered to return that property, with a warning that anyone who caused further trouble would be severely punished. Apparently, the king personally resolved this property dispute in the area of Jungseong-ri and had his judgment inscribed on a stele to ensure that such disputes would not occur again.

131
Myeonghwalsanseong Fortress Stele

Bomun-dong, Gyeongju
Silla, 511 CE
H. 66.8 cm

132
Namsansinseong Fortress Stelae

Namsan Mountain, Gyeongju
Silla, 591 CE
H. 91.0 cm (Stele No. 1)

The stelae from Namsansinseong Fortress record the construction of the fortress in 591 (thirteenth year of King Jinpyeong), including information about local officials and residents who participated in the construction. To date, ten such stelae have been discovered, all of which begin with the following sentence: "Upon the completed construction of Namsansinseong Fortress on the twenty-sixth day of the second month of the '*Sinhae*' year (591), let it be widely known and pledged that if the fortress should collapse within three years of this date, it will be deemed by law as a crime." The place names in the listed titles of officials correspond to present-day locations such as Gyeongju, Haman, Okcheon, Yeongju, and Goseong. According to the stelae, the total circumference of Namsansinseong Fortress was approximately 2,800 *bo* (步, a traditional unit of measurement). Each local group was responsible for constructing a section of the fortress ranging in length from 7 *bo* and 8 *cheok* (尺, approximately 30 cm) to 21 *bo* and 1 *cheok*, suggesting that at least 200 groups were mobilized for the construction.

No.1

No.3

No.5

No.6

No.4

No.9

No.7

No.8

Official Recognition of Buddhism and the Building of Temples

After originally being transmitted to Silla in the fifth century, Buddhism was recognized as the official religion during the reign of King Beopheung (r. 514–540), following the martyrdom of Ichadon in 527 or 528. The Silla royal family actively embraced Buddhism, and Buddhist ideas and beliefs permeated the lives of the Silla people. Numerous temples were built in Gyeongju, including the "Seven Temple Sites" ("*Chilcheo garam*"), which comprise Heungnyunsa, Yeongheungsa, Hwangnyongsa, Bunhwangsa, Yeongmyosa, Cheonwangsa, and Dameomsa. King Jinheung completed the construction of Heungnyunsa, Silla's first temple, in 544, and oversaw the construction of Hwangnyongsa from 553 to 566. In 574, a large Buddha statue called "Jangyukjonsang" was enshrined in Hwangnyongsa Temple. Queen Seondeok (r. 632–647) built Bunhwangsa Temple, which means "Fragrant Temple of the Emperor," next to Hwangnyongsa Temple in 634. Then from 643 to 645, a nine-story wooden pagoda was built at Hwangnyongsa Temple to represent the queen's majesty and petition the Buddha for help in facing a national crisis.

133
Stele Commemorating the Martyrdom of Ichadon

Dongcheon-dong, Gyeongju
Unified Silla, 817 / 818 CE
H. 106 cm

Buddhism was officially accepted as the national religion of Silla under King Beopheung, after Ichadon was martyred in 527 or 528. It is written in *Samguk yusa* (*Memorabilia of the Three Kingdoms*) that when Ichadon was beheaded, milky white blood gushed out from his neck, his head fell on Geumgangsan Mountain, and flowers rained down from the sky.

This stele has six sides, one of which features a relief carving of Ichadon's martyrdom. The remaining five sides record King Beopheung's will to widely disseminate Buddhism, a conversation between Ichadon and King Beopheung, the conflict between the king and his subjects over the official recognition of Buddhism, and Ichadon's death. Hence, this stele has great historical and religious importance in documenting the official recognition of Buddhism, which had a profound influence on Silla society and culture, in both images and text.

• Heungnyunsa Temple

The place that was once thought to be the site of Heungnyunsa Temple, Silla's first Buddhist temple, was officially designated as a historic site. However, later research at the site uncovered a roof tile with the inscription "靈廟之寺" ("Temple of Yeongmyo") and a convex roof-end tile decorated with a design of a human face, indicating that it was actually the former site of Yeongmyosa Temple. Meanwhile, a roof tile with an inscription associated with Heungnyunsa was found on the grounds of Gyeongju Industrial High School, suggesting that this might be the true site of Heungnyunsa Temple.

134
Roof Tile with Inscription: "興"

Sajeong-dong, Gyeongju
Unified Silla
L. 10.7 cm

135
Roof-end Tiles

Sajeong-dong, Gyeongju
Silla-Unified Silla
D. 15.3 cm (top left)

136
Bodhisattva Head
Hwangnyongsa Temple Site (presumed), Gyeongju
Silla, 7th century CE
H. 8.3 cm

• Hwangnyongsa Temple

Hwangnyongsa Temple, the largest and most important temple in Silla, was home to two of the three treasures of Silla mentioned in *Samguk yusa*: a sixteen-foot bronze Buddha statue and the temple's nine-story wooden pagoda. According to legend, in 553 (fourteenth year of King Jinheung), a yellow dragon appeared during the construction of a palace east of Wolseong Fortress in Gyeongju. As a result, the plans for the palace were scrapped and a temple named Hwangnyongsa was instead built on the site. Under King Jinheung (r. 540–576), the foundations of the temple were laid, the temple walls were built, and the sixteen-foot bronze Buddha statue was installed. The main halls were built in 584 under King Jinpyeong (r. 579–632), and the nine-story wooden pagoda was erected during the reign of Queen Seondeok (r. 632–647). Through the centuries, the nine-story wooden pagoda tilted or burned multiple times, including when the entire temple was destroyed by fire during the Mongol invasion of 1238. Whenever the pagoda was reconstructed, additional sarira reliquaries were newly enshrined in the pagoda, alongside the previously enshrined reliquaries. One of the sarira caskets was engraved on both the inside and outside with the "Records of the Construction and Renovation of the Wooden Pagoda at Hwangnyongsa Temple," which contains detailed information on how the nine-story wooden pagoda was repaired and rebuilt in 872 (twelfth year of King Gyeongmun). During the reconstruction projects, various offerings were placed beneath the central foundation stone of the pagoda, including a white porcelain jar, various vessels, fine metalwork ornaments, and beads.

137
Roof-end Tiles with Lotus Design
Hwangnyongsa Temple Site, Gyeongju
Silla-Unified Silla
D. 18.5 cm (bottom right)

138
Chimi
(Ridge-end Roof Tile)

Hwangnyongsa Temple Site, Gyeongju
Silla
H. 182.0 cm

"*Chimi*" are special roof tiles that were placed at both ends of the main roof ridge of a wooden building. In addition to stabilizing the ridge and protecting against fire, *chimi* served a decorative function, enhancing the aesthetic beauty of the building, and were also believed to repel evil spirits. This is the largest extant example of a *chimi* roof tile in Korea, and it comes from Hwangnyongsa Temple. The upper and lower sections of this *chimi* were made separately and then joined together via "ㄱ"-shaped and "ㄴ"-shaped grooves on each upper and lower section.

The sides and back are decorated with designs of lotuses and human faces. One of the male faces has a beard, clearly distinguishing it from a female face.

Detail of Face Pattern

139
Stone Cover of the Sarira Chamber
Central Foundation Stone of the Wooden Pagoda Site at Hwangnyongsa Temple, Gyeongju
Silla, 645 CE
L. 44.3 cm

140
Sarira Outer Casket (North Side)
Central Foundation Stone of the Wooden Pagoda Site at Hwangnyongsa Temple, Gyeongju
Silla, 645 CE
L. 26.0 cm

141

Silver Plates with Inscriptions from the "Ye Dhamma Formular"

Central Foundation Stone of the Wooden Pagoda Site at
Hwangnyongsa Temple, Gyeongju
Unified Silla
L. 8.0 cm (left)

These silver plates are inscribed with lines from the "Ye Dhamma Formular" ("Pratītyasamutpāda gāthā"), or "Incantation of Dependent Origination." Lines from the same source have also been found on a brick with a pagoda design from the site of Seokjangsa Temple in Gyeongju and on the outer surface of a sarira casket enshrined within the five-story stone pagoda at Bowonsa Temple in Seosan.

142

Sarira Reliquaries

Wooden Pagoda Site at Hwangnyongsa Temple, Gyeongju
Silla-Unified Silla
H. 13.6 cm (bronze bowl with lid)

143

Silver Bowl with Lid

Central Foundation Stone of the Wooden Pagoda Site at
Hwangnyongsa Temple, Gyeongju
Silla-Unified Silla
H. 4.5 cm

144

Octagonal Sarira Case

Central Foundation Stone of the Wooden Pagoda Site at Hwangnyongsa Temple, Gyeongju
Unified Silla
H. 12.3 cm

145

Square Case · Cylindrical Case

Central Foundation Stone of the Wooden Pagoda Site at Hwangnyongsa Temple, Gyeongju
Silla-Unified Silla
H. 6.1 cm (left)

146

Octagonal Sarira Case

Central Foundation Stone of the Wooden Pagoda Site at Hwangnyongsa Temple, Gyeongju
Unified Silla
D. 10.0 cm (left)

147

Lotus-shaped Pedestal

Central Foundation Stone of the Wooden Pagoda Site at Hwangnyongsa Temple, Gyeongju
Silla-Unified Silla
H. 3.0 cm

• Yeongmyosa Temple

Yeongmyosa Temple was founded in 635 by Silla's Queen Seondeok. It later became the home of the Divine Bell of King Seongdeok the Great, which was moved to Yeongmyosa in 1460 by King Sejo of the Joseon Dynasty. Excavations at the site of Yeongmyosa uncovered roof tiles inscribed with the name of the temple and a roof-end tile decorated with a smiling human face, which is the only one of its kind ever discovered. The smiling face of the person, which has become an iconic symbol of Silla, looks quite natural, rather than artificial. Although this roof-end tile is only partially intact, traces of a semi-cylindrical convex roof tile on the back indicate that it was actually used on a Silla building.

148
Roof Tiles with Inscription: "令妙寺(靈廟寺)"
Gyeongju
Goryeo
L. 19.0 cm

149
Roof-end Tile with Human Face Design
Yeongmyosa Temple site, Gyeongju
Unified Silla
L. 11.5 cm
Treasure

- **Bunhwangsa Temple**

More than twenty temples were built during the reign of Queen Seondeok (r. 632–647), the most notable of which is Bunhwangsa Temple in Gyeongju, which was built in 634. It is said that Bunhwangsa Temple was once the residence of the famous monks Jajang and Wonhyo, and also featured a mural of the thousand-armed Avalokiteshvara painted by Solgeo, as well as a Bhaishajyaguru Buddha statue made during the reign of King Gyeongdeok. Bunhwangsa is also home to the oldest stone brick pagoda in Korea, which was made by cutting stones into rectangular plates or tiles, which were then stacked like bricks. The pagoda is estimated to have originally had seven or nine stories, although only three stories remain today.

A stone sarira casket was discovered between the second and third tiers of the stone brick pagoda, which was found to contain sarira reliquaries of silver and glass and an array of other offerings, including gilt-bronze ornaments, beads, shells, and coins.

150
Stone Lion
Bunhwangsa Temple, Gyeongju
Unified Silla, 8th century CE
H. 85.0 cm

151
Sarira Casket

Stone Brick Pagoda at Bunhwangsa Temple, Gyeongju
Silla, 634 CE
Total H. 72.0 cm

This granite sarira casket was discovered between the second and third tiers of the stone brick pagoda at Bunhwangsa Temple when the pagoda was being dismantled for repairs in 1915. The body of the casket was made by flattening and polishing the top of a natural stone and then hollowing out a square cavity for the sarira reliquaries and other offerings. A hole was drilled on one side of the base to allow rainwater to drain out. Several protrusions were made around the upper edge to keep the lid securely in place. The lid of the casket was finished with greater care than the body, with the sides cut at diagonals with rounded edges.

152
Ornaments

Stone Brick Pagoda at Bunhwangsa Temple, Gyeongju
Silla-Unified Silla
L. 25.7 cm (bottom left)

153
Sarira Reliquaries

Stone Brick Pagoda at Bunhwangsa Temple, Gyeongju
Silla, 645 CE-Goryeo 12th century CE
L. 8.4 cm (top right)

154
Brick with *Go* Board Design

Bunhwangsa Temple, Gyeongju
Unified Silla
L. 43.0 cm
Gyeongju National Research Institute of Cultural Heritage

The floors and walls of some Silla buildings were covered with bricks or tiles such as this, which feature a variety of designs and patterns. Bricks from the Unified Silla period are often adorned with lotus or floral medallion designs, but designs of dragons, Buddha statues, and pagodas have also been found. This brick, excavated from Bunhwangsa Temple, is etched with a grid of fifteen vertical columns and fifteen horizontal rows, which was likely used to play *go*. The game of *go* seems to have been quite popular in Silla, as evidenced by hundreds of *go* stone pieces that have been found at various Silla sites dating to the fifth century, including the tombs of Hwangnamdaechong, Geumgwanchong, and Jjoksaem 44.

Territorial Expansion and Final Unification of the Three Kingdoms

After establishing and stabilizing its centralized government under King Jijeung and King Beopheung, Silla began expanding its territory under King Jinheung (r. 540–576). Most crucially, King Jinheung gained control of the Han River basin, which opened the way for direct trade and interaction with the dynasties of China. Bolstered by the economic power provided by this region, Silla steadily extended its control over the Korean Peninsula, laying the groundwork for the unification of the Three Kingdoms. Silla's active territorial expansion in this period is evidenced by multiple stele monuments commemorating King Jinheung's inspection tours of newly conquered lands in various regions, as well as the presence of Silla tombs throughout the central and southern parts of the peninsula.

In the ensuing years, Silla faced constant counterattacks from Goguryeo and Baekje, which led to several national crises. However, with military support from China's Tang Dynasty, Silla's King Muyeol (r. 654–661) defeated Baekje in 660, and then his son King Munmu (r. 661–681) vanquished Goguryeo in 668. In 676, King Munmu expelled Tang forces from the Korean Peninsula, creating a unified state. He then reorganized the governance system to better serve the new nation, and embraced the people and cultures of Goguryeo and Baekje, laying the foundation for Korean culture.

155
Necklace
Cheonbu-dong, Ulleung
Unified Silla, 7th-8th century CE
D. 0.7-1.2 cm

• Subjugating the Usanguk Polity

King Jijeung asserted his control over areas that were deemed as possible military threats by reorganizing their administrative system and dispatching his own provincial administrators. For example, he sent a military general named Isabu to Siljikguk (present-day Samcheok, Gangwon-do Province) to defend the east coast against Goguryeo invasions. Then in 512, Isabu was sent to subjugate Usanguk (present-day Ulleungdo Island) in the East Sea. Attesting to Silla's expansion along the east coast, Silla-style pottery and necklaces were recovered from stone chamber tombs in Cheonbu-dong, Ulleungdo, and Silla pottery was found in tombs in Chodang-dong and Byeongsan-dong, Gangneung.

156
Silla Style Pottery
Chodang-dong, Gangneung
Three Kingdoms,
6th century CE
H. 30.3 cm (back row, center)

157
Geumgwan Gaya Style Pottery
Samgye-dong, Gimhae
Three Kingdoms, 6th century CE
H. 28.0 cm (back row, center)

• Consolidating Geumgwan Gaya

Located at the mouth of the Nakdong River (present-day Gimhae, Gyeongsangnam-do Province), Geumgwan Gaya long controlled maritime trade along sea routes leading to regions controlled by the dynasties of China, as well as to the Wa people of the Japanese Archipelago. But after being attacked by the combined forces of Silla and Goguryeo in 400, Geumgwan Gaya went into decline in the fifth century, and was ultimately annexed by Silla in 532 when King Guhae of Geumgwan Gaya (r. 521–532) surrendered to Silla's King Beopheung. Hence, large amounts of Silla pottery have been discovered at sites in Gimhae from after the fifth century, including mounted dishes with alternating perforations and long-necked mounted jars.

158
Silla Style Pottery
Samgye-dong, Gimhae
Three Kingdoms, 6th century CE
H. 25.7 cm (back row, center)

• Conquering Dae Gaya

After the late fourth century, Dae Gaya, supported by Baekje, emerged as the most powerful of the Gaya polities. By the late fifth and early sixth century, Dae Gaya had expanded its territory to span from the western areas of Yeongnam to the eastern areas of Honam, even amid struggles with neighboring powers. Then in 554, Dae Gaya, launched an attack on Silla alongside King Seongwang of Baekje (r. 532–554), who was attempting to regain control of the Han River basin. After being defeated in this conflict, Dae Gaya quickly declined before falling to King Jinheung in 562.

159
Dae Gaya Style Pottery
Jisan-dong, Goryeong
Three Kingdoms, 6th century CE
H. 21.5 cm (far left)

160
Silla Style Pottery
Jisan-dong, Goryeong
Three Kingdoms, 6th century CE
H. 28.9 cm (back row, center)

- Claiming the Han River Basin

During the Three Kingdoms period, the Han River basin was an area of great geographical and military importance. Baekje was the first to settle in the Han River basin, where they flourished throughout the fourth century. But in 475, Baekje lost the region to Goguryeo following Goguryeo's southern campaigns. Later, Silla and Baekje formed an alliance against Goguryeo, and in 551, their combined forces attacked and seized the Han River basin. They divided the territory, with Silla taking the upper reaches of the Han River and Baekje claiming the lower reaches. Three years later, however, Silla attacked Baekje and took control of the lower reaches as well. By establishing Sinju Province in the region, Silla was able to exert total control over the Han River basin, giving them access to direct trade routes with China and paving the way for the unification of the Three Kingdoms.

161
Excavated Artifacts from Nuam-ri Tomb
Nuam-ri, Chungju
Silla, 6th century CE
H. 16.8 cm (bottom left)

162
Excavated Artifacts from Seongdong-ri Tomb
Seongdong-ri, Paju
Silla, 6th century CE
H. 31.2 cm (back row, center)

163
Stele of the Tomb of King Munmu

Dongbu-dong, Gyeongju (Discovered in 2009)
Unified Silla, 681-682 CE
H. 60.0 cm

This stele commemorates the achievements of King Munmu. The inscription was written by Kim □□, who held the post of "Gukhak sogyeong," and transcribed in calligraphy by Great Monk Hannulyu. The text contains genealogical information about the Silla royal family, and documents King Munmu's achievements, his will, and the process of his funeral. For many years, this stele was thought to be lost, being known only through ink rubbings of the inscription. However, the lower part of the stele was found in 1961, and the upper part was found in 2009.

164
Stele of the Tomb of King Munmu (bottom part)

Dongbu-dong, Gyeongju (Discovered in 1961)
Unified Silla, 681-682 CE
H. 55.1 cm

165
Zodiac Figure (Pig)
Tomb Attributed to Kim Yu-sin
Unified Silla, 7th-8th century CE
H. 40.8 cm

Bas-relief sculptures carved from soapstone and depicting zodiac figures (such as a horse, pig, and rabbit) were excavated from the perimeter of the Tomb of General Kim Yu-sin. This figure of a pig, which has the head of a boar and a human body, stands with its feet apart on a rock, striking a regal pose. The body is realistically depicted wearing an elaborate and ornately decorated suit of armor with long sleeves of fluttering fabric that convey a distinct sense of life. Based on their overall appearance, the sculptures from the Tomb of General Kim Yu-sin are estimated to be the oldest Silla zodiac figures in existence.

Buddhist Temples for Protecting the State

The people of Silla strongly believed in the power of Buddhism to protect the state, and thus commonly engaged in patriotic projects and practices known as "*hoguk*" (state-protection) Buddhism. One of the best-known examples is the construction of Sacheonwangsa Temple under King Munmu. It is said that, when the Tang Dynasty of China invaded Silla in 670 (tenth year of King Munmu), the monk Myeongrang built a temporary temple at the foot of Nangsan Mountain, with walls made from colored silk and statues of grass. By practicing his secret arts there, Myeongrang conjured a mighty storm at sea that sunk the Tang fleet. Thus, Sacheonwangsa Temple was later constructed at the same site. Another example is Gameunsa Temple on the East Sea, which King Munmu began constructing in order to protect the country from Japanese pirates. However, King Munmu died before the temple was finished, so his son King Sinmun (r. 681–692) took over the construction. After cremating his father and scattering his remains in the East Sea, King Sinmun completed Gameunsa Temple in his father's honor in 682. Notably, the East and West three-story pagodas of Gameunsa Temple are the first twin stone pagodas erected after Silla's unification. Two Sarira reliquaries of similar form were found within these twin structures.

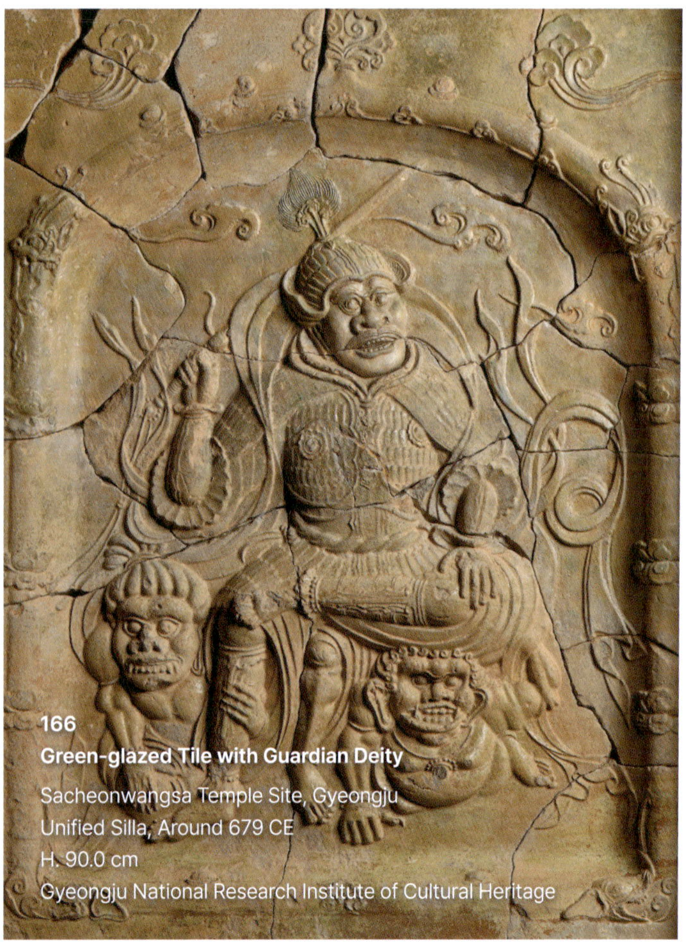

166
Green-glazed Tile with Guardian Deity
Sacheonwangsa Temple Site, Gyeongju
Unified Silla, Around 679 CE
H. 90.0 cm
Gyeongju National Research Institute of Cultural Heritage

• Sacheonwangsa Temple

Sacheonwangsa Temple was built by King Munmu in 679, at a time when tensions were rising between Silla and the Tang Dynasty following the unification of the Three Kingdoms. Notably, the temple was constructed in Sinyurim Forest on Nangsan Mountain in Gyeongju, a place that had long been held sacred in the local tradition. Following its construction, Sacheonwangsa became the center of "Buddhism to Protect the State." As the first temple in Korea to feature twin pagodas and a single main hall, Sacheonwangsa established the standard layout for many future Silla temples, including Gameunsa Temple (682), Mangdeoksa Temple (685), Bulguksa Temple, and the temple at Cheongun-dong (both built in the eighth century).

The east and west pagodas were built on square foundations with three bays per side, with a square sarira chamber in the central foundation stone. These green-glazed wall tiles with relief images of the guardian deities once decorated the pedestals of the east and west wooden pagodas at Sacheonwangsa Temple. Each pagoda featured twenty-four such tiles (six per side), which were arranged at regular intervals around the pedestal, separated by pillars and stacks of vine-patterned bricks. Three different guardian deities are depicted on the extant tiles. According to *Samguk yusa*, the Silla monk Yangji, who was a master sculptor, participated in the creation of images of the Eight Legions that adorned the bases of the pagodas at Cheonwangsa Temple. This suggests that the monk Yangji was also the creator of the guardian deity's images.

167
Green-glazed Tile with Guardian Deity
Sacheonwangsa Temple Site, Gyeongju
Unified Silla, Around 679 CE
H. 90.0 cm
Gyeongju National Research Institute of Cultural Heritage

168
Roof Tiles with Inscription: "四天王寺"
Sacheonwangsa Temple Site, Gyeongju
Unified Silla-Goryeo
L. 25.0 cm (back row, right)

169
Green-glazed Bricks
Sacheonwangsa Temple Site, Gyeongju
Unified Silla
L. 28.0 cm (top)
Gyeongju National Research Institute of Cultural Heritage

170
Roof-end Tiles
Sacheonwangsa Temple Site, Gyeongju
Unified Silla-Goryeo
W. 27.0 cm (back row, right)
Gyeongju National Research Institute of Cultural Heritage

171

Outer Sarira Casket · Inner Sarira Casket · Sarira Bottle

West Three-story Stone Pagoda at Gameunsa Temple Site, Gyeongju

Unified Silla, Around 682 CE

H. 16.5 cm (inner casket)

Treasure

- Gameunsa Temple

Gameunsa Temple was built by King Sinmun (r. 681–692) around 682, shortly after Silla's unification of the Three Kingdoms, to pray for the repose of his late father, King Munmu. A pair of matching three-story stone pagodas remain standing at the site of Gameunsa Temple, each of which was found to contain similar sarira reliquaries. In 1959, when the west pagoda was dismantled for repairs, elaborate sarira reliquaries were found in a cavity on the upper surface of the third-story body stone. The reliquaries consisted of a small crystal sarira bottle that was placed atop an inner sarira casket shaped like a pavilion, covered by a bowl-shaped lid with a sculpted lotus and a large gem. This inner sarira casket was then placed inside a box-shaped outer sarira casket featuring images of the Four Heavenly Kings, who protect Buddha and the Buddhist teaching.

The inner casket features four celestial musicians respectively arranged on the four corners of the pavilion. It once included a roof cover and railings, but they were badly damaged and could not be restored to their original state. On the outer casket, the relief images of the Four Heavenly Kings have very natural postures, created with delicate carving techniques. These vivid images, along with the various decorations that were made separately and then attached to the reliquary, demonstrate the advanced nature of Silla metalwork technology.

top

West facing in situ

South facing in situ

172
Outer Sarira Casket

West Three-story Stone Pagoda
at Gameunsa Temple Site, Gyeongju
Unified Silla, Around 682 CE
H. 28.0 cm
Treasure

V.

Golden Age of Silla Culture

After the unifying the Three Kingdoms and expelling the Tang Dynasty, Silla entered a period of political stability based on a strong royal authority, which allowed their culture to flourish. By embracing styles and practices from both Goguryeo and Baekje and adopting cultural advancements from the Tang, Silla developed into an elaborate and sophisticated civilization. This civilization reached its peak during the reign of King Seongdeok (r. 702–737), when the Tang Dynasty recognized Silla as a "Country of Gentlemen" and praised its cultural achievements.

Buddhism remained the dominant ideology, spreading from the royal capital through the provinces. This period saw the creation of the greatest masterpieces of Silla Buddhist culture, including Bulguksa Temple, Seokguram Grotto, and the Divine Bell of King Seongdeok the Great. Large temples were constructed, with the layout of two pagodas in front of the main hall being widely adopted. Quintessential examples of the stone pagodas from this era include the east and west three-story stone pagodas of Gameunsa Temple site and the three-story stone pagoda of Bulguksa Temple. By combining Tang stylistic influences with Silla aesthetics, Buddhist sculpture reached new heights, resulting in innovative works with superb proportions. Buddhist crafts also thrived, highlighted by large bells and sarira reliquaries, showing tremendous technical skill and sculptural beauty.

Following unification, extravagant new facilities like Wolji Pond were built in the royal capital, which became a splendid cosmopolitan city that attracted people not only from the neighboring regions of China and Japan, but also merchants from as far away as Arabia. The construction of royal tombs became more systematic, reflecting the increasing power of the monarchy. Memorial stelae were erected, and statues of scholars, warriors, and lions were placed along the tomb paths. Tomb mounds were further adorned with statues of zodiac figures and stone railings, marking the completion of the Silla style of royal tombs. Cremation was also practiced during this period, reflecting the influence of Buddhism.

Flourishing of Buddhist Culture

After Buddhism was recognized as the official religion of Silla, many temples were built in Gyeongju, as evidenced by a line in *Samguk yusa* that reads, "There were many temples like stars and pagodas lined up like geese" (寺寺星張 塔塔雁行). Following the construction of Heungnyunsa Temple in Cheonkyungrim Forest, temples were established around Wolseong Fortress in the mid-sixth century, around Namsan and Nangsan Mountains in the late seventh century, and in the Tohamsan Mountain area and throughout the outskirts of Gyeongju from the eighth century onward. The royal family established an organization called "Seongjeon" to manage, maintain, and operate the major temples, including conducting state ceremonies.

After the unification of the Three Kingdoms, Buddhism became even more popular and widespread, with new temples being built not only in the capital, but also in the provinces. People of all classes participated in the establishment of these new temples, from the royal family and aristocrats to the local gentry and commoners. From the eighth century onward, *Mugujeonggwang Daedarani gyeong* (*Great Dharani Sutra*) came to be regarded as a significant text, having a considerable influence on Buddhist faith and the construction of pagodas. As Buddhism took deep root in the Silla society, Buddhist culture flourished, reaching its zenith during the Unified Silla period.

173

Divine Bell of King Seongdeok the Great

Bongdeoksa Temple, Gyeongju
Unified Silla, 771 CE
H. 365.8 cm
National Treasure

This bell was originally hung in Bongdeoksa Temple, which was dedicated to King Seongdeok (r. 702–737). After the temple fell into ruins, the bell was moved to several different locations: first to Yeongmyosa Temple in Gyeongju, then to the former site of the Gyeongju National Museum in Dongbu-dong (outside the South Gate of the Gyeongju Fortress), and finally to its current location at Gyeongju National Museum in 1975. The bell takes its name from the first line of its inscription, found in the center of the body, which reads, "聖德大王神鍾之銘" ("Inscription of the Divine Bell of King Seongdeok the Great"). The bell also bears a poem praising Silla for unifying the Three Kingdoms, as well as the names of those who contributed to its production.

Designated as a National Treasure, the bell is considered to be one of the most beautiful and distinguished of all Korean bells. Its impeccable form, intricately carved designs, and clear, majestic sound are renowned not only in Korea, but worldwide. The main body features several striking and vibrant carvings of figures, including a donor holding a censer with a handle. With its sculptural elegance, flawless casting technique, and spiritual resonance, the Divine Bell of King Seongdeok the Great is revered as one of the finest Buddhist artworks of its time.

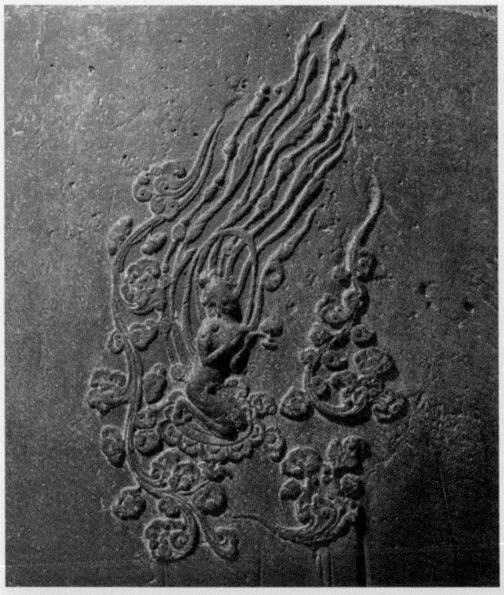

detail

174
Vajrapani

Seokguram Grotto, Gyeongju
Unified Silla, 8th century CE
H. 55.0 cm

This is the head of a Vajrapani statue that was discovered when Seokguram Grotto underwent repairs during the period of Japanese occupation. The back of the head is flat, indicating that it was once attached to a wall. The raised left arm and lowered left hand have also survived, allowing one to imagine the appearance of the full figure. Although only parts of the statue remain, the vivid three-dimensional expression truly captures the divine strength of the Vajrapani, demonstrating a level of sculptural expertise befitting the reputation of Seokguram Grotto.

皇龍寺刹柱本記

• Inner Sarira Casket of the Nine-story Wooden Pagoda of Hwangnyongsa Temple and Records of its Construction and Renovation

The sarira receptacle within the central foundation stone of the nine-story wooden pagoda of Hwangnyongsa Temple yielded both an outer sarira casket and an inner sarira casket. The inner casket was a gilt-bronze box made from four separate plates, along with a lid. According to an inscription found on six of the box's inner and outer sides, this inner casket was enshrined in 872 (twelfth year of King Gyeongmun) during a repair of the pagoda. The inscription, which is entitled "*Chalju bongi*," also provides information about the origin of the central pillar (or "*chalju*") of the wooden pagoda, the pagoda's original construction in 645, King Gyeongmun's reasons for and process of rebuilding of the pagoda, and the contents of the sarira reliquaries.

175

Inner Sarira Casket (Records of the Construction and Renovation of the Wooden Pagoda at Hwangnyongsa Temple)

Central Foundation Stone of the Wooden Pagoda Site at Hwangnyongsa Temple, Gyeongju
Unified Silla, 872 CE
L. 22.5 cm (each)

Inner side

Outer side

Outer side

Inner side

176

Inner Sarira Casket Lid

Central Foundation Stone of the Wooden Pagoda Site at
Hwangnyongsa Temple, Gyeongju
Unified Silla, 872 CE
L. 27.0 cm

Detail of Inner Sarira Casket Lid

177
Sarira Reliquary with Inscription: "仲和三年"

Wooden Pagoda Site at Hwangnyongsa Temple, Gyeongju
Unified Silla, 883 CE
H. 17.0 cm

• Saria Reliquary with Inscription: "Third Year of Zhonghe"

This cylindrical container was among the sarira reliquaries found in the nine-story wooden pagoda of Hwangnyongsa Temple. Based on its inscription, this container seems to be some type of sarira reliquary, which was enshrined for Kim Yu-sin in a large stone pagoda of a temple associated with him. However, these details do not correspond to its eventual discovery in the wooden pagoda of Hwangnyongsa Temple. Thus, it is believed that this container was consecrated in a related temple in 883 (third year of the Zhonghe era), before later being moved to Hwangnyongsa Temple. It might also have simply been mingled with various sarira reliquaries (including some from Hwangnyongsa) that were confiscated after having been looted.

178
Hip-end Roof Tile with Lotus Design

Hwangnyongsa Temple Site, Gyeongju
Unified Silla
L. 45.7 cm

179
Brick with Floral Medallion Design
Temple Site to the West of Hwangnyongsa Temple, Gyeongju
Unified Silla
L. 33.5 cm
Gyeongju National Research Institute of Cultural Heritage

180
Bricks with Floral Medallion and Dragon Design
Hwangnyongsa Temple Site, Gyeongju
Unified Silla
L. 36.8 cm

181
Eight Legions (Garuda and Kinnara)

Changrimsa Temple Site, Gyeongju
Unified Silla, 9th century CE
H. 88.0 cm (right)

During the Unified Silla era, the pedestals of stone pagodas typically featured carvings of the deities of the Eight Legions: Deva, Naga, Yaksha, Gandharva, Asura, Garuda, Kinnara, and Mahoraga. In Buddhist lore, the Eight Legions were one of various groups that gathered to hear the sermons of the Buddha, and they are often depicted in Buddhist artworks listening to and protecting the Buddha's teachings. The deities on these two pedestal stones are Garuda and Kinnara. In ancient Indian folklore, Garuda is a divine bird that lives in the sky and eats dragons with its powerful beak, while Kinnara is a deity who sings and dances. In this depiction, there is a bird sitting atop Kinnara's head, as well as a cow and horse on either side of its face. Both Garuda and Kinnara are wearing and fluttering robes while sitting on clouds, which was the typical iconography for images of guardian deities.

182
Roof Tiles with Inscription: "昌林寺"

Changrimsa Temple Site · Cheongwansa Temple Site, Gyeongju
Unified Silla-Goryeo
L. 17.5 cm (right)
Gyeongju National Research Institute of Cultural Heritage

183
Brick with Buddha Design

Gapsansa Temple Site, Gyeongju
Unified Silla
L. 8.6 cm

This tile decorated with a Buddha triad is inscribed with the name "Gapsansa Temple." Interestingly, no temple with that name is mentioned in either *Samguk yusa* or *Samguk sagi*, making this tile the only evidence of its existence. The tile, which likely decorated a wall or floor of the temple, is filled with a carving of a Buddha flanked by two bodhisattvas and other Buddhist images. Both the Buddha and bodhisattvas are characterized by their elongated bodies, and the nimbus and hems of the garments were expressed in a delicate and natural manner.

184
Roof Tiles with Inscription: "甲山寺"

Cabsansa Temple Site, Gyeongju
Goryeo
L. 27.7 cm (right)

185
Small Votive Pagodas

Temple Site in Inwang-dong, Gyeongju
Unified Silla, 8th century CE
H. 10.8 cm (right)
Gyeongju National Research Institute of Cultural Heritage

186
Stone-carved Sutra

Chilbulam Temple, Gyeongju
Unified Silla
L. 12.0 cm

187
Sarira Case

Dongcheon-dong, Gyeongju
Unified Silla, 9th century CE
H. 9.3 cm

In addition to handwritten and printed manuscripts, Buddhist sutras were also carved into stone to be handed down through the generations. Since they could be preserved for many years, stone-carved sutras often became objects of worship. This stone fragment, which was discovered at Chilbulam Temple in Gyeongju, contains part of a passage from the *Diamond Sutra*, which reads: “All appearances are false. If you realize that appearances are not appearances, you will see the Tathagata.”

This box-shaped sarira case was discovered in 1964 in a stone casket that was buried on the slope of Yaksan Mountain in Dongcheon-dong, Gyeongju. The lid is decorated with a floral design around the central knob, while each side of the body has been engraved with images of the Four Heavenly Kings, protectors of Buddhism, in thin lines.

188
Sutra Case

Namsan Mountain (presumed), Gyeongju
Unified Silla
H. 3.9 cm

This sutra case, which was reportedly found on Namsan Mountain in Gyeongju, contained two copies of the *Incantation of Wish-Fulfillment Amulet*, one written in Sanskrit and the other in Chinese characters, which are the oldest versions of that text ever found in Korea. The case is made from copper and has a removable lid, and both sides of its walls were gilded and then engraved with various designs using thin lines. The case shows many of the characteristic details of gilt-bronze sarira reliquaries of the Unified Silla period, including the overall manufacturing technique, the borderline along the sides conveying the appearance of a three-dimensional edge, the style of the floral medallion designs and images of the guardian deities, and the dot pattern filling in the background space. Such details can also be seen on gilt-bronze sarira caskets from Seokgatap Pagoda in Bulguksa Temple and the five-story stone pagoda from the temple site in Nawon-ri, both in Gyeongju.

Buddhist Sculpture and Art

Buddhist statues and scriptures were first introduced to the Korean Peninsula during the Three Kingdoms period, around the same time that Buddhism itself was introduced. After Buddhism was accepted in Silla, numerous statues were created according to the needs and preferences of people of the time. Stone Buddha statues began to be produced in the seventh century and remained popular throughout the Unified Silla period. In particular, many large and small Buddha statues were carved on Namsan Mountain in Gyeongju. The people of Silla believed that Buddhism would protect their nation from outside threats, a belief that is vividly reflected in its statues of Buddhist guardian deities, who are typically depicted wearing armor and holding weapons to subdue demons. Silla produced diverse images of a wide range of guardian deities, who are lower in status than Buddhas and bodhisattvas, including representations of the Vajra Warriors, the Four Heavenly Kings, and the Eight Legions. Their intense expressions, muscular physiques, and dynamic postures embody their role as protectors of Silla, the land of Buddha.

189
Infant Buddha

Nonsan
Silla, 7th century CE
H. 10.7 cm

190
Pensive Bodhisattva

Seonggeon-dong, Gyeongju
Silla, 7th century CE
H. 14.1 cm

191
Pensive Bodhisattva

Songhwasan Mountain, Gyeongju
Silla, 7th century CE
H. 125.0 cm

This pensive bodhisattva statue was brought to the museum in 1930 from Geumsanjae, the ritual shrine of the Tomb of General Kim Yu-sin on Songhwasan Mountain in Gyeongju. The figure sits on a chair with the right leg raised and stretched across the left knee, while the left foot rests on a lotus flower. The head and arms are missing, but the upper torso remains, wearing only a necklace. The lower body is covered by a skirt with wavy wrinkles in the lower hem. This is one of the representative stone pensive bodhisattva statues of Silla, along with the one from Bukji-ri, Bonghwa, which is now housed at Kyungpook National University Museum.

192
Maitreya Triad

Jangchanggok Valley, Namsan Mountain, Gyeongju
Silla, 7th century CE
H. 167.0 cm (center)
Treasure

This set of three sculptures of a Buddha and two bodhisattvas was discovered in 1924 in a stone chamber in Jangchanggok Valley, Namsan Mountain, Gyeongju. With their remarkably delicate details and soft expressions carved from solid granite, they are representative works of Silla sculpture. The central Buddha is seated on a chair, with the left hand holding the robe on the left knee and the right palm facing outward over the right knee, with the fingers slightly bent. The enlarged proportion of the head, childlike appearance, and innocent facial expression are all characteristics of Silla Buddhist statues from the seventh century. The two bodhisattvas show many of the same sculptural details as the Buddha, although the decorative details and positions of the hands are different. These two figures are sometimes affectionately known as "Baby Buddhas" because of their size and cute expressions. This triad is presumed to represent the "Maitreya of Samhwaryoung Pass," who is mentioned in the account of the Maitreya of Saengeuisa Temple in *Samguk yusa*.

193
Buddhist Plaques (Buddha Triad, Bodhisattva)

Donggung Palace and Wolji Pond, Gyeongju
Unified Silla, 7th century CE
H. 21.3 cm (top)
Treasure

194
Buddha Triad

Donggung Palace and Wolji Pond, Gyeongju
Unified Silla, late 7th century CE
H. 27.0 cm
Treasure

The Buddha sits in the center atop a lotus pedestal in the lotus position, with his hands gathered in front of his chest and his thumbs and index fingers touching. This hand gesture, known as the preaching mudra, symbolizes the transmission of the Buddha's teachings to the world. The Buddha's robe is draped over both shoulders. The Buddha is flanked by two bodhisattvas, who turn to face him. The composition and iconography resemble the Amitabha Pure Land Mural made in China in the 7th century and the Amitabha Triad and Two Monks Plaque made in Japan in the late 7th to early 8th century. Thus, this Buddha triad plaque from Wolji Pond reflected the latest trends in East Asian Buddhist art.

• Buddhas with abhaya-vara mudra

These Buddha figures have right hands raised with the palm facing outward, forming the abhaya mudra symbolizing relief from fear and anxiety, and left hands lowered with the palm facing outward, forming the vara mudra symbolizing the granting of wishes. Many Buddha statues depict the hands in these two positions, showing that the Buddha frees all living beings from fear and grants their wishes. These hand positions have appeared in Korean Buddhist sculpture from early times, and remained popular throughout the Three Kingdoms period and Unified Silla period.

195
Buddha
Provenance Unknown
Unified Silla, 8th century CE
H. 22.3 cm

196
Buddha
Provenance Unknown
Unified Silla, 8th century CE
H. 21.6 cm

197
Buddha

Provenance Unknown
Unified Silla, 9th century CE
H. 29.0 cm

These two Buddha statues, which have a similar form, are the largest of the gilt-bronze Buddha statues excavated from Wolji Pond. The bodies and pedestals were made separately and then joined together, and they also originally featured a backing nimbus, which is now missing. Both heads feature a high *ushnisha*, but one of them is plain and the other is adorned with tight curls. The rounded faces have closed eyes and lines representing the eyebrows, and the large ears are curved like bows. Each figure has three folds around the neck, and their hands are forming the *abhaya* and *vara* mudras. They stand atop octagonal pedestals shaped like lotus flowers, with open horizontal ovals around the bottom, a detail known as the "*ansang* pattern," and leaf-shaped decorations extending upward. Judging by the style of the garments and the leaf decorations, these statues are estimated to have been made in the late eighth century.

198
Buddhas

Donggung Palace and Wolji Pond, Gyeongju
Unified Silla, Late 8th century CE
H. 35.0 cm (right)

199
Buddhas

Dongqung Palace and Wolji Pond, Gyeongju
Unified Silla, 8th-9th century CE
H. 21.0 cm (top left)

• Vairocana Buddha

Vairocana Buddha is a symbol of truth, who is often used to visualize the Buddhist reverence for teaching and the *dharma*. As seen here, sculptures of Vairocana Buddha often form the "wisdom-fist" mudra, with one hand wrapped around the raised index finger of the other hand, held in front of the chest. While Vairocana images from China and Japan generally depict the figure as a bodhisattva, those from Silla have the appearance of a Buddha.

200
Vairocana Buddha
Provenance Unknown
Unified Silla, 8th century CE
H. 39.7 cm

201
Vairocana Buddha
Provenance Unknown
Unified Silla, 9th century CE
H. 31.5 cm

Bhaishajyaguru Buddha was believed to cure all diseases, extend life, and benefit every aspect of human life. This large statue of Bhaishajyaguru Buddha, with a height of nearly 180 cm, is highly regarded for its outstanding sculptural beauty. Indeed, it is considered one of the three representative gilt-bronze Buddha statues of Unified Silla, along with the Amitabha Buddha and Vairocana Buddha of Bulguksa Temple in Gyeongju. The two hands, which were made separately and attached to the arms, have been lost, but the figure is presumed to be Bhaishajyaguru Buddha based on the position of the raised arms.

The back of the statue shows evidence of Silla's advanced technique for making large sculptures, wherein molten metal was poured over a clay model of the sculpture inside a mold. After the metal hardened, the inner clay model was then removed through large holes in the crown, head, and back of the statue. Some of the edges of the holes have slight ledges, indicating that a finishing plate was inserted. There are also traces of a device that was used to affix the outer and inner molds together at regular intervals on the body.

202
Bhaishajyaguru Buddha

Baengnyulsa Temple, Gyeongju
Unified Silla, about 800 CE
H. 179.0 cm
National Treasure

Rear

• Bodhisattvas

Bodhisattvas are benevolent beings who have attained or will attain enlightenment, yet dedicate their lives to teaching and helping all living beings before becoming Buddha. In Buddhist images, bodhisattvas are typically shown wearing jeweled crowns, beautiful garments, and opulent accessories, and often holding lotuses, vases, or beads in their hands. Some of the most revered bodhisattvas include Manjushri, the symbol of wisdom; Samantabhadra, the symbol of practice and meditation; Avalokiteshvara, the incarnation of compassion; Maitreya, the foreordained Buddha of the future who teaches living beings; and Kshitigarbha, who helps save living beings in times when there is no Buddha.

203
Bodhisattva
Dong-gu, Daegu
Unified Silla, 8th century CE
H. 11.7 cm

204
Bodhisattva
Sangju
Unified Silla, 8th century CE
H. 13.0 cm

205
Eleven-faced Avalokiteshvara

Nangsan Mountain, Gyeongju
Unified Silla, 8th century CE
H. 200.0 cm

This statue, which was originally found near the site of Jungsaengsa Temple on Nangsan Mountain in Gyeongju, depicts the eleven-faced Avalokiteshvara Bodhisattva. According to tradition, the bodhisattva has three faces looking forward, which are merciful and save those who are good; three faces on the left, which are angry and save those who are evil; three faces on the right, which encourage the righteous to be more diligent; and one smiling face on the back that imbues all beings with laughter. However, some eleven-faced Avalokiteshvara statues from the Unified Silla period do not follow this iconography.

This bodhisattva has ten miniature heads forming a band around the main head, along with an elaborate necklace and a long beaded ornament that extends from the shoulders down past the knees. The right hand is raised below the chest, and the lowered left hand is holding a water bottle. This statue is believed to have been made in the eighth century, during the golden age of Silla Buddhist sculpture.

206

Buddhist Ornamental Plaques

Donggung Palace and Wolji Pond, Gyeongju
Unified Silla, 8th century CE
L. 4.0-10.0 cm

Excavations at the sites of Donggung Palace and Buildings 2 to 4, which are part of the Wolji Pond complex, yielded numerous ornamental plaques depicting Buddhist figures and motifs, which were likely used to decorate the nimbuses of Buddhist statues and gilt-bronze banners. These ornaments include single and triad Buddha images, flying apsaras, guardian deities, celestial canopies, jewels, and scenes of the division and distribution of sarira. The single Buddhas have very rudimentary facial features, and are often depicted beneath a celestial canopy. There are also paired images of Buddha with another figure with palms pressed together in reverence, and triad compositions, all but one of which show the figures seated and riding on clouds beneath a celestial canopy. Among the scenes of the division and distribution of sarira, three unusual examples have been identified: two ornaments feature a three-story pagoda being carried on the backs of elephant and horse, while another shows a figure with palms pressed together seated on an elephant. The most common type of ornament in this group depicts flying apsaras, which also happen to be the most popular motif for decorating the nimbuses of Buddha statues. A large number of jewel-shaped ornaments were also unearthed. Most feature rock crystal inlaid over cloud motifs, evoking the splendid imagery of the celestial realm.

207
Buddha

Inwang-dong, Gyeongju
Silla, 7th century CE
H. 112.0 cm

209
Buddha

Wangjeonggok Valley, Namsan Mountain, Gyeongju
Unified Silla, 8th century CE
H. 201.0 cm

208
Bhaishajyaguru Buddha

Nangsan Mountain, Gyeongju
Unified Silla
H. 128.5 cm

210
Buddha

Gyeongjueupseong Walled Town, Gyeongju
Unified Silla, 8th century CE
H. 175.0 cm

Most stone Buddhist statues in Korea are made from granite, but this one was carved from a softer stone. The statue also has a very unique appearance, with a voluptuous body and three-dimensional folds in the garments, conveying an exotic sensibility. It seems to match the style of Buddhist statues from the Tang Dynasty (618–907) of China, which in turn show the influence of Buddhist statues from the Gupta period (third to sixth century) of India. Thus, this statue attests to Silla's exchange with other countries and adoption of new styles.

211
Buddha

Osangye Valley, Namsan Mountain, Gyeongju
Unified Silla, 9th century CE
H. 172.7 cm

212
Bhaishajyaguru Buddha
Yongjanggok Valley, Namsan Mountain, Gyeongju
Unified Silla, late 8th-9th century CE
H. 305.0 cm

This Buddha statue once stood in Yongjanggok Valley, Namsan Mountain in Gyeongju. It was partially fragmented, but after being brought to the museum, pieces of the head and nimbus were reattached to restore the statue to its current appearance. Bhaishajyaguru is a Buddha who cures all diseases, extends life, and benefits every aspect of human life. The figure holds a medicine jar in its left hand, while the right hand forms the "earth-touching" mudra.

There is a hemispheric *ushnisha* atop the rounded face, and the garment reveals the right shoulder. The Buddha's head and body are surrounded by a nimbus filled with engraved vine patterns, with embossed flames along the edges. Based on the relatively static nature of the body and the highly decorative nature of the nimbus patterns, this statue is estimated to have been made in the late eighth or ninth century, during the Unified Silla period.

213
Avalokiteshvara Bodhisattva

Nangsan Mountain, Gyeongju
Unified Silla, 9th century CE
H. 376.0 cm

Avalokitesvara Bodhisattva is typically depicted wearing a jeweled crown adorned with a miniature Buddha figure and holding a water bottle. Although the crown on this statue is heavily worn, making it difficult to discern the miniature Buddha, the figure can still be identified as Avalokiteshvara Bodhisattva by the bottle in the left hand. The head of the statue was discovered and brought to the museum during the period of Japanese occupation, and the body was later found half-buried near the site of Neungji Pagoda at the western foot of Nangsan Mountain in Gyeongju. It was later determined that the two pieces were from the same statue. In 1997, the lotus pedestal was discovered near the site where the body had been found, and the statue was reassembled into its current form.

214
Buddha Head

Cheolwagol Valley, Namsan Mountain, Gyeongju
Unified Silla, late 8th-early 9th century CE
H. 153.0 cm

215
Vajrapanis
Ha-dong, Gyeongju
Unified Silla
H. 84.0 cm

216
Vajrapanis
Temple Site in Guhwang-dong, Gyeongju
Unified Silla, 7th century CE
H. 143.0 cm (left)

Vajrapani is a deity indigenous to India, who was regarded as a guardian of Buddha and his teachings from the advent of Buddhism. East Asian images of Vajrapani often depict a pair of the deities, one with an open mouth, which is said to represent "*Ah*" (阿), the first letter in the Sanskrit alphabet, and the other with a closed mouth representing the last letter, "*Hum*" (吽). These are two of eight stone panels featuring Vajrapani images that once decorated the four sides of the first floor of a stone pagoda. Four more of the Vajrapani panels still remain at the temple site in Guhwang-dong, Gyeongju. These panels likely flanked the open niches on each side of the stone pagoda, as seen on the stone brick pagoda of Bunhwangsa Temple.

217

Four Heavenly Kings

Gyeongjueupseong Walled Town, Gyeongju
Unified Silla, 8th century CE
H. 83.0 cm

The Four Heavenly Kings are guardian deities who protect the Buddha's teachings, and who are believed to reside on the slopes of Mt. Sumeru, located at the center of the world, each guarding one of the four cardinal directions. On this stone from a pagoda, the Four Heavenly Kings are wearing armor and fluttering robes while standing on clouds or stepping on evil spirits. Vaisravana (guardian of the north) is holding a pagoda, while Dhrtarashtra (guardian of the east), Virudhaka (guardian of the south), and Virupaksha (guardian of the west) all hold swords. All of the figures have a powerful appearance, exemplifying their roles as the divine protectors of Silla, the land of Buddha.

218
Three-story Stone Pagoda

Goseonsa Temple Site, Gyeongju
Unified Silla, Before 686 CE
H. 10.1 m
National Treasure

The three-story stone pagoda from the site of Goseonsa Temple is composed of eighty-two stones and stands 10.1 meters tall. With the exception of the doorway carved into the body of the first story, it is almost identical to the east and west three-story stone pagodas at Gameunsa Temple, built in 682 (second year of King Sinmun), showing the characteristic form of Unified Silla stone pagodas. Goseonsa Temple was located in Amgok-dong, Gyeongju, around the upper reaches of Alcheon Stream, but this site was submerged after the construction of Deokdong Dam in 1975. Thus, prior to the submersion, the pagoda was relocated to the museum, along with a stele base and several long rectangular stones from the site.

219
Three-story Stone Pagoda
Seungsogol Valley, Namsan Mountain, Gyeongju
Unified Silla, 9th century CE
H. 377.0 cm

220
Three-story Stone Pagoda
Samneung, Namsan Mountain, Gyeongju
Unified Silla
H. 216.0 cm

221
Stone Lantern
Gyeongjueupseong Walled Town, Gyeongju
Unified Silla, 8th-9th century CE
H. 259.0 cm

222
Stone Lantern
Gyeongjueupseong Walled Town, Gyeongju
Unified Silla, 8th-9th century CE
H. 221.0 cm

Sarira Reliquaries from the Late Unified Silla Period

After the eighth century, the sarira reliquaries enshrined in the temples of the Silla capital and provinces became simplified. The number of nested sarira reliquaries in a set decreased, with only the outer casket and sarira bottle being used in many cases, and the types and quantities of offerings also decreased. In the early eighth century, the influence of *Mugujeonggwang Daedaranigyeong* (*Great Dharani Sutra*) began to grow, and its guidelines for decorating sarira and making pagodas were actively embraced by Silla (even before being adopted by China), eventually becoming widespread by the late Unified Silla period. As stated in the *Great Dharani Sutra*, whenever a pagoda is constructed or repaired, miniature pagodas containing copies of the sutra should be enshrined within, and anyone who does this will accumulate merit. Thus, many Silla pagodas have been found to contain copies of the *Great Dharani Sutra* and small votive pagodas, either together or separate. The miniature pagodas were sometimes enshrined in sets of seventy-seven or ninety-nine pieces, although fewer pieces were used in other cases.

223

Sarira Reliquaries-Sarira Jar · Sarira Bottle · Votive Pagodas

East Three-story Stone Pagoda at Seodong-ri, Bonghwa
Unified Silla, 9th century CE
H. 9.1 cm (jar)

When the east three-story stone pagoda at Seodong-ri in Bonghwa-gun was dismantled for repairs, sarira reliquaries were discovered in the center of the sarira chamber carved in the top of the body stone of the first floor. The reliquaries included a round jar made from soapstone, which contained a glass sarira bottle, and ninety-nine miniature terracotta pagodas. The pagodas have holes on the bottom where rolled copies of *dharani* written in ink were likely once placed, and some of the holes still have wooden stoppers.

224
Sarira Reliquaries-Votive Pagoda · Sarira Jar · Sutra Case

Three-story Stone Pagoda at the Chukseosa Temple, Bonghwa
Unified Silla, 867 CE
L. 24.1 cm (front)

These sarira reliquaries were at Chukseosa Temple until 1929, when they were purchased by a Japanese person before being sold again to the Joseon Government-General Museum. At present, only a stone sarira jar, cylindrical sutra case, and one terracotta votive pagoda remain. Inscriptions on the outer surface of the sarira jar record the year that the pagoda was built and the sarira jar was enshrined, and also provide information about the person who made the offering and its purpose. In particular, the inscription, along with the presence of the pagoda and sutra case, confirms that these reliquaries were produced and enshrined as part of the "Mugujeong pagoda" faith, which was popular at the time. There is a prominent hole in the side of the stone sarira jar, the purpose of which is unknown.

225
Sarira Reliquaries-Sarira Jars · Pagoda Stone Tablet Records

Three-story Stone Pagoda at the Beopgwangsa Temple Site, Pohang
Unified Silla, 9th century CE
H. 10.8 cm (far right)

These reliquary items, which were found together, consist of a round soapstone jar inscribed with *Buljeongjonsung Dharani* (*Sutra of the Victorious Buddha-Crown*), a bronze sarira jar, and two stone tablets that record details of the pagoda's construction. The soapstone jar is the oldest artifact from Unified Silla with a confirmed date. One of the two stone tablets was also produced during the Unified Silla period, while the other was enshrined much later, during the Joseon period. The inscription on the Unified Silla tablet states that its stone pagoda was built in 828 and moved in 846 (eighth year of King Munseong). It also records that, at the time of the pagoda's construction, the benefactor of Beopgwangsa Temple was Kim Gyunjeong, the father of King Sinmu (forty-fifth king of Silla), which shows that Beopgwangsa Temple flourished through the support of the Silla royal family. The Joseon stone tablet reports that the temple underwent repairs in 1698 and the pagoda was repaired in 1747.

Revision of Governance System and Social Changes

As its territory grew, Silla enacted a series of measures to reorganize its system of governance and stabilize the country. First, it established the Gukhak, which was a higher learning institution that trained prospective government officials in Confucian principles and administrative practices. Once installed as bureaucrats in government positions, the Gukhak alumni typically promoted policies that strengthened royal authority.

Various political offices were created or reorganized to expand the functions of the bureaucracy. For example, the Seongjeon department was established to oversee maintenance, repairs, and services at major temples, a role that the government had never filled prior to unification. The inscription on the Divine Bell of King Seongdeok the Great, which was completed in 771, documents the offices and titles of those who participated in its manufacture, providing a glimpse into how the Seongjeon operated.

In addition, Silla also established a standardized measuring system for collecting taxes and trading goods, seeking to eliminate inconsistencies in length, volume, and weight. In fact, according to *Samguk sagi*, King Munmu readjusted the standard measurement for one bolt of silk and hemp cloth in 665, while his kingdom was at war with the Tang Dynasty, indicating that such inconsistencies must have been a very important social and economic issue. State rituals also became more standardized as the former regions of Baekje and Goguryeo were incorporated into the Silla ritual system. Thus, following unification, Silla went to great lengths to reorganize many different aspects of its governance system.

Training Bureaucrats and Document-based Administration

One of Silla's top priorities was to train new government officials to work for the newly unified state. In particular, prospective bureaucrats needed to be well-versed in Confucianism, which was the prevailing ideology of the time. For this purpose, the Gukhak was established as Silla's premier educational institution, providing instruction in Confucian classics, such as the *Analects*, as well as writing and other administrative practices. The discovery of wooden tablets containing passages from the *Analects* at sites in Gimhae and Incheon, quite a distance from Gyeongju, confirms that education in Confucianism took place not only in the Silla capital, but also in the provinces.

After completing their studies at the Gukhak, students were appointed as bureaucrats in the expanding government, where they needed to show their capacity in document-based administration. The use of documents increased after unification as Silla sought to effectively manage its vastly enlarged state, as demonstrated by the discovery of inkstones excavated in various regions, including Gyeongju. In 675, King Munmu ordered the production and distribution of official copper seals for government offices, provinces, and counties, signaling the full implementation of an administrative bureaucracy relying on documents.

Stele of the Tomb of King Munmu

The inscription featured on the Stele of King Munmu begins with the passage that Kim□□, who held the post of "Gukhak sogyeong," composed the inscription by royal command. The most important educational institution in Silla was the Gukhak, which was first established under Queen Jindeok (r. 647–654), through the influence of the Tang Dynasty, before being finalized and fully instituted under King Sinmun in 682. The primary purpose of the Gukhak was to train future government officials in Confucianism. As such, the curriculum focused on Confucian texts such as the *Analects, Book on Filial Piety, and the Book of Changes*. Literature was also taught to help students gain proficiency in writing, preparing them for government service in the new document-based bureaucracy.

At Gaeseonsa Temple in Damyang, there is a stone lantern that was made in 868 to honor King Gyeongmun (r. 861–875), Empress Mooneui, and the "Great Princess," who later became Queen Jinseong (r. 887–897). Designated as a Treasure, the stone lantern features inscriptions that record the date and process of its construction. One of the passages from the inscription, which concerns the expense of oil used to light the lanterns, mentions the name "Sagan Kim Joongyong, former Gukjagam gyeong." "Gukjagam" means "Gukhak," indicating that the two terms were used interchangeably in Silla, while "gyeong" was the title of the head supervisor of the Gukhak.

Stone Lantern of Gaeseonsa Temple in Damyang

Gyeongju Hyanggyo, built on the site of Silla's Gukhak (photograph from the period of Japanese occupation)

226
Clay Figure

Yonggang-dong, Gyeongju
Unified Silla, 8th century CE
H. 17.1 cm

In 648, Kim Chunchu (who later became King Taejong Muyeol, r. 654–661) implemented the Tang-style of official dress for Silla royals and bureaucrats. The robes of Silla officials changed accordingly, as demonstrated by free-standing sculptures, known as "*toyong*", of court officials that were excavated from a stone chamber tomb in Yonggang-dong, as well as segments of a bronze belt recovered from the site of Donggung Palace and Wolji Pond. Although the *toyong* figure appears to have the facial features of a person from West Asia, he is wearing the robes of a Silla bureaucrat and holding a court tablet, conjuring the image of Silla officials standing in formation during assemblies or state events.

227

Belt Pieces

Donggung Palace and Wolji Pond, Gyeongju
Unified Silla
L. 5.4 cm (far left)

228

Official Seal

376, Hwangnam-dong, Gyeongju
Unified Silla
L. 3.2 cm

229

Official Seal

681-1, Dongcheon-dong, Gyeongju
Unified Silla
L. 3.5 cm

After unifying the Korean Peninsula, Silla expanded its bureaucratic organization and enforced state control through document-based administration grounded in codes and regulations. Thus, bureaucrats were required to carry seals, which they kept on their person at all times, that were used to guarantee the authenticity of official documents. Demonstrating this, a seal excavated from the Hwangnam-dong 376 site in Gyeongju bears the imprint of the word "*gwanin*," meaning "official seal."

First Side Second Side Third Side

230

Wooden Slip Document

Donggung Palace and Wolji Pond, Gyeongju
Unified Silla, 8th-9th century CE
L. 31.9 cm

This wooden slip features writing on three sides. The text on the second side is mostly indecipherable, making it difficult to understand the full meaning, but the identity of the sender and receiver, as well as the partial date, can be discerned. The message seems to have been sent on the "twenty-seventh day of the twelfth month" from a person named Sarim, who held the post of "Jeondaesa," to two government offices. Hence, this wooden slip evinces the increasing use of documents in Silla's government administration, allowing us to envision the duties and practices of bureaucrats working in central government offices. The method of recording the date and author of the document at the end of the text follows the format of documents described in the codes and regulations of the Tang Dynasty and ancient Japan.

231
Inkstones

Gyeongju
Unified Silla
H. 10.2 cm (top right)

Many inkstones with multiple legs have been found at the sites of Silla palaces. Some of them have the heads of animals carved on the legs, enhancing their practical function with a decorative touch.

232
Lacquerware Inkstone

Donggung Palace and Wolji Pond, Gyeongju
Unified Silla, 8th-9th century CE
L. 15.0 cm

The wood was carved to hold an inkstone, which features black-lacquered edges. The sides were finished with needle fir, while a different species was used for the inner part where the inkstone was inserted. The use of black-lacquer around the edges indicates that this was a highly luxurious inkstone. It is the only extant lacquered inkstone in Korea, and given the wear of the well where the ink pooled, it appears to have been used over a long period of time.

233

Inkstone with Inscription: "椋司"

Donggung Palace and Wolji Pond, Gyeongju
Unified Silla, 8th-9th century CE
D. 16.5 cm

The bottom of this inkstone is inscribed in ink with the word "椋司" ("*gyeongsa*"). A "*gyeong*" was a type of elevated warehouse structure that was raised off the ground on pillars. Thus, "*gyeongsa*" likely refers to an office overseeing such a warehouse, which apparently owned and used this inkstone.

234

Large Jar with Inscription: "十石入瓮"

Donggung Palace and Wolji Pond, Gyeongju
Unified Silla, 8th century CE
H. 150.0 cm

In Unified Silla, the official units for measuring volume were *hop*, *doe*, *mal*, and *seom*. Ten *hop* equaled one *doe*, ten *doe* equaled one *mal*, and ten *mal* equaled one *seom*. The inscription on this jar means a "jar that holds 10 *seom*." It was previously thought that one *seom* equated to around 52 liters, meaning that this jar would have held 520 liters, but more recent analyses have suggested that the jar may actually hold 721 liters. Because of its inscription, this jar is an important resource for studying the measurement systems of Silla.

Inscription Detail

Rituals

In ancient times, people believed that rituals were an essential practice that could determine the future of the country. Thus, one of the duties of Silla royals and officials was to perform such rituals, which were often dedicated to ancestors or the heavens. After the unification of the Three Kingdoms, this practice took on even greater significance, with official rituals being regularly conducted at the royal ancestral shrine and altars to deities of grains and the earth, as well as for mountains and streams.

Since Gyeongju is located on an alluvial fan, the area has an unusually large number of wells. In Silla, these wells were regarded as vital sources of the life force, which not only provided drinking water, but also served as conduits through which the will of the heavens was transmitted. Accordingly, various rituals were performed at wells to ensure national stability and prosperity, to heal illnesses, to ward off evil spirits, or to overcome drought. Excavations of well sites in and around Gyeongju have yielded an array of artifacts related to rituals, including a wooden tablet inscribed with the words "龍王" ("Dragon King"), lead scissors, bronze vessels, pottery, and animal bones. The animal bones are believed to be the remains of food or sacrificial offerings used in well rituals, while the inscribed tablet helps to visualize how rituals to the Dragon King were performed at wells in the Silla era.

235
Pottery and Wooden Tools Excavated from an Well
Inwang-dong, Gyeongju
Unified Silla
L. 29.5 cm (front row bucket)

236
Wooden Slip with Inscription
Inwang-dong, Gyeongju
Unified Silla
L. 24.1 cm

First Side Second Side

237
Comb
Inwang-dong, Gyeongju
Unified Silla
L. 10.3 cm

238
Dog Bones
Hwangnam-dong, Gyeongju
Unified Silla
L. 18.1 cm (far left)

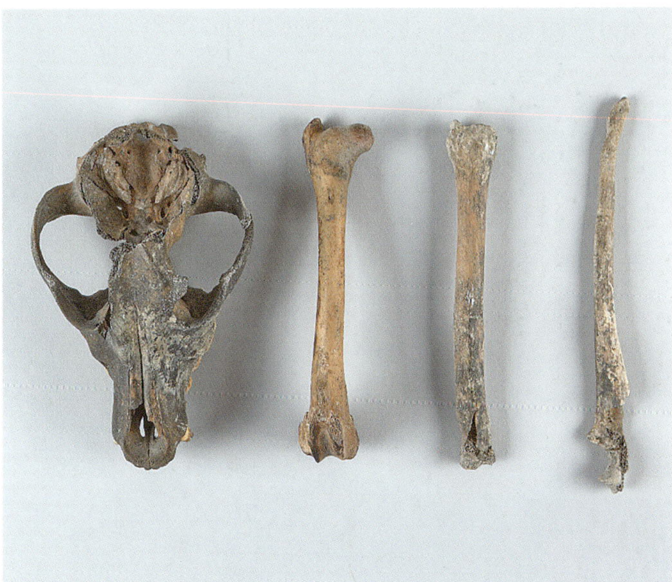

239
Bronze Vessels · Bronze Spoon · Bronze Hairpins
Inwang-dong, Gyeongju
Unified Silla
D. 7.0 cm (dish)

240
Pottery with Inscription: "辛審龍王"

Donggung Palace and Wolji Pond, Gyeongju
Unified Silla, 8th-9th century CE
D. 19.9 cm

241
Pottery with Inscription: "辛審龍王"

Donggung Palace and Wolji Pond, Gyeongju
Unified Silla, 8th-9th century CE
D. 11.4 cm

Excavations at the sites of Donggung Palace and Wolji Pond in Gyeongju uncovered several pieces of pottery bearing the inscription "辛審龍王" ("*sinshim yongwang*"), which are believed to have been used in rituals dedicated to the Dragon King ("*yongwang*"). Donggunggwan, which was the government office that managed Donggung Palace and Wolji Pond, included a department called Yongwangjeon, which seems to have been responsible for overseeing the Dragon King rituals held at Wolji Pond.

242
Censer Lid
Donggung Palace and Wolji Pond, Gyeongju
Unified Silla, 8th-9th century CE
H. 16.5 cm

This lion figurine, made from high-quality stone, served as the lid of an incense burner. The lid would be placed over a container of burning incense, allowing the smoke to emerge through holes in the lion's throat and nostrils. Decorative incense burners like this are thought to have been used in ceremonies and rituals held at the royal court.

243
Scissors

Donggung Palace and Wolji Pond, Gyeongju
Unified Silla, 8th-9th century CE
L. 7.3 cm (bottom)

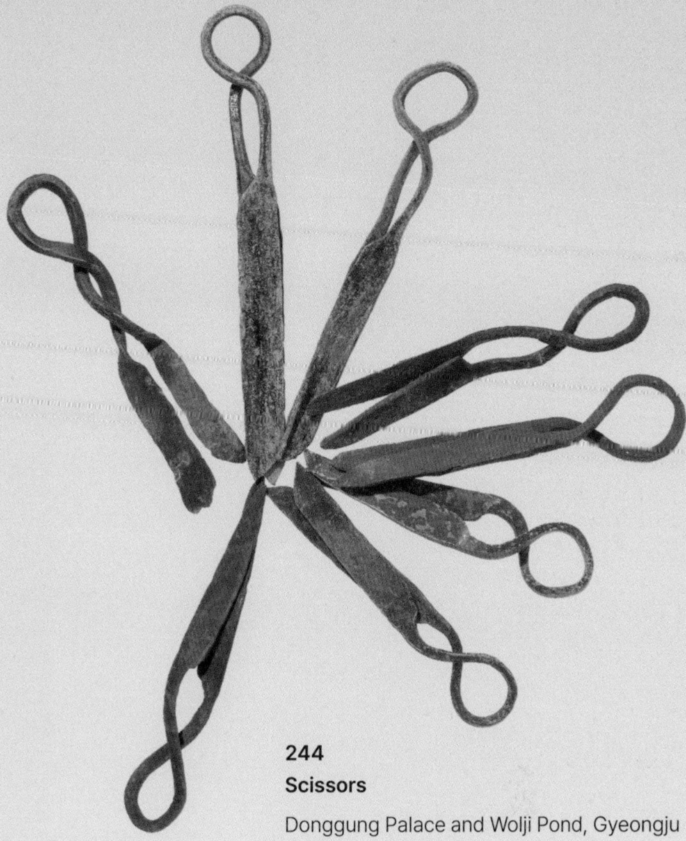

244
Scissors

Donggung Palace and Wolji Pond, Gyeongju
Unified Silla, 8th-9th century CE
L. 13.0 cm (top center)

245
Round Plates

Donggung Palace and Wolji Pond, Gyeongju
Unified Silla, 8th-9th century CE
D. 12.5 cm (top left)

Maintenance of the Royal Capital

As the capital of Silla, the city of Gyeongju, which was then called Geumsung, was the center of the kingdom's politics, economy, culture, and defense. Once Silla established its capital in Gyeongju, it was never relocated. The flow of goods and products through the capital steadily increased over time, as did its political power. This is evidenced by records in *Samguk sagi* documenting road repairs and the creation of relay stations in 487, and the establishment of a market in the royal capital in 509.

Early on, tombs for the royal family and aristocracy were built in the center of the capital, creating a unique landscape. But starting in the first half of the sixth century, new tombs were moved to the outskirts of the capital, in areas such as Seoak-dong and Bomun-dong. Instead, Buddhist temples, including Heungnyunsa Temple, were built within the capital. By the late seventh century, every approach to the capital was lined with large temples, evoking the image of Gyeongju as the land of Buddha.

Beginning in the mid-sixth century, parts of the capital were subdivided by a grid system of roads, maximizing land use. From the eighth century onward, this grid system expanded throughout the capital, extending from the area north of Bukcheon Stream to the area south of Namcheon Stream. Roads with three different widths have thus far been identified in the road system of Silla's capital—more than 15 meters wide, around 10 meters wide, and around 5 meters wide—indicating that the size of the roads was also systematically planned.

Unification of the Three Kingdoms and Major Civil Works

After unifying the Korean Peninsula in 668, Silla enacted various projects aimed at showcasing the power of the newly enlarged state to both domestic and international observers. Thus, as recorded in *Samguk sagi*, the Silla palace underwent lavish renovations in 679, including the construction of Donggung Palace, and various gates inside and outside the palace were named. Moreover, the efforts to convey the might and majesty of the unified dynasty extended beyond the palace to other areas of the capital, as demonstrated by tiles inscribed with the phrase "儀鳳四年皆土" ("*uibongsanyeon gaeto*"). "*Uibongsanyeon*" refers to the fourth year of the Yifeng era (679), while "*gaeto*" is believed to denote a major civil engineering project. Such tiles have been found throughout Gyeongju, including around Wolseong Fortress, suggesting the massive scale of redevelopments at that time.

The unification of the Three Kingdoms also significantly increased the population of Silla, including in the capital, where the space for residential expansion was somewhat limited. To address such constraints, King Sinmun attempted to move the capital to Dalgubeol (present-day Daegu) in 689, but his plan failed due to opposition from the aristocracy. Instead, King Sinmun began earnestly developing the area north of Bukcheon Stream, such as Dongcheon-dong. With all of these major civil projects taking place, the demand for roof tiles surged from the late seventh century onward. In conjunction with this increase, the designs on convex roof-end tiles, which had previously been dominated by lotus motifs, became more diverse, while the base clay used to make roof tiles became coarser than in earlier periods.

246
Roof-end Tile with Lotus Design

Donggung Palace and Wolji Pond, Gyeongju
Unified Silla, late 7th century CE
D. 13.3 cm

Starting in the second half of the seventh century, many roof-end tiles were decorated with the design of a lotus flower with two layers of petals, encircled by a band of dots. Although this design was more elaborate than the lotus motifs on earlier roof-end tiles, the motifs were still expressed with almost perfect symmetry, creating a sense of harmony and balance. Roof-end tiles with this lotus design are representative of the late seventh century, having been excavated at Donggung Palace, Wolji Pond, and Sacheonwangsa Temple, all of which were built around 679.

247

Roof Tile with Inscription: "儀鳳四年皆土"

Donggung Palace and Wolji Pond, Gyeongju

Unified Silla, 679 CE

L. 39.2 cm

Detail

248

Roof-end Tiles

Gyeongju

Unified Silla

L. 35.3 cm (top right)

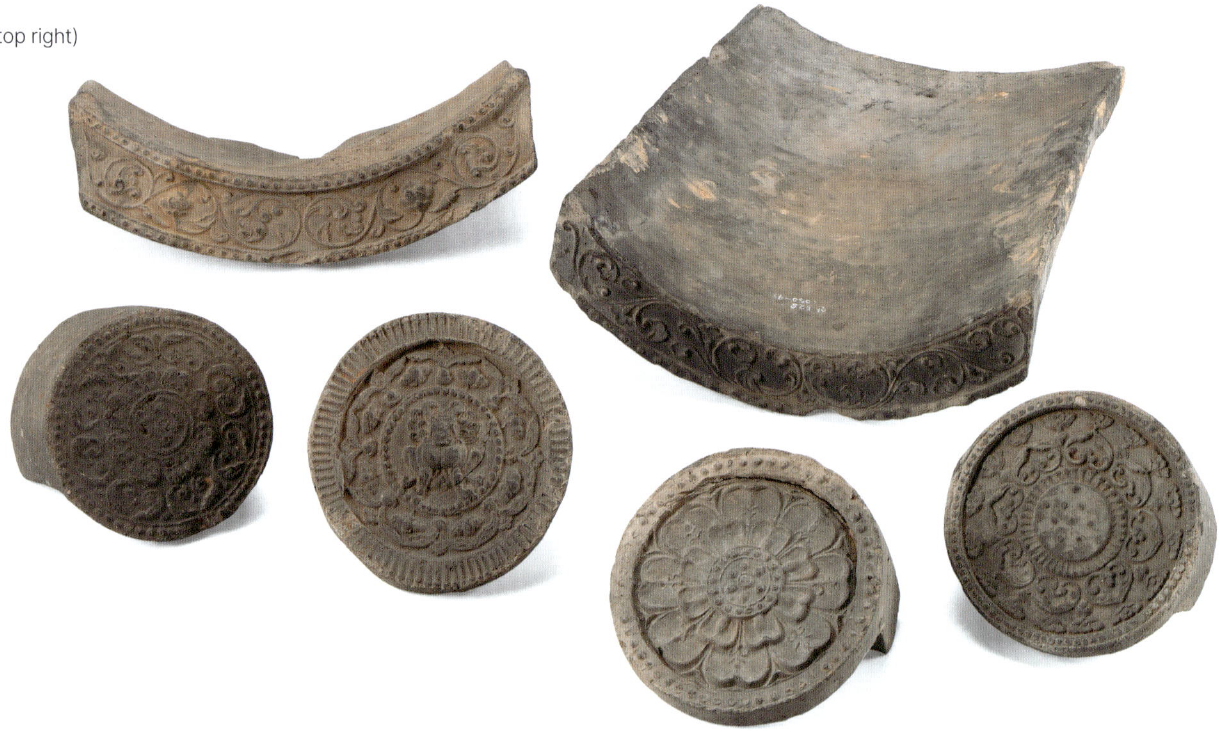

249

Roof-end Tiles with Lotus Design

Hwangnyongsa Temple Site, Gyeongju · Heungnyunsa Temple Site (presumed), Gyeongju
Unified Silla
D. 13.2 cm (right)

250

Roof-end Tiles with Animal Design

Donggung Palace and Wolji Pond, Gyeongju
Unified Silla, 8th-9th century CE
D. 14.2 cm (left)

251

Roof-end Tile with Inscription: "在城"

Donggung Palace and Wolji Pond, Gyeongju
Unified Silla, 8th-9th century CE
D. 16.9 cm

Roof tiles inscribed with "在城" ("*jaeseong*"), meaning "fortress where the king resides," have been discovered in the area of Wolseong Fortress in Gyeongju. Tiles with the same inscription have also been found at the site of a roof-tile kiln in Geumjang-ri, indicating that tiles for the royal palace were produced at this site.

252

Roof-end Tiles and Roof Tiles with Inscription: "在城"

Donggung Palace and Wolji Pond, Gyeongju
Unified Silla, 8th-9th century CE
D. 15.5 cm (left)

253
Brick with Dragon and Building Designs

Temple Site in Jungsan-dong, Ulsan
Unified Silla
L. 15.4 cm

This brick was discovered at a temple site in Jungsan-dong, Ulsan, during the period of Japanese occupation. It features an unusual design of a dragon and some type of building that was presumably used at the time. The dragon and building appear on four sides of the brick, each occupying about half the surface, with only half of the building being expressed.
However, another brick was found with a design showing two similar buildings in their entirety, revealing more details. One side of the brick is decorated with a scene of two buildings on a high pedestal, with clouds in the background. The buildings have three bays in the front, and many other details can also be identified, including the doors, bars on the windows, and the structure above the pillars. The eaves of the roof point upwards to the sky, and there are decorative ridge-end roof tiles (*chimi*) at both ends of the central ridge, which curve sharply inwards. Artifacts that show the shape and characteristics of wooden buildings from the time, such as this brick and fragments of a house-shaped pottery vessel found at the site of Sacheonwangsa Temple in Gyeongju, are quite rare, and provide valuable information about the architectural styles of Silla.

254
Brick with Building Design

Temple Site in Jungsan-dong, Ulsan
Unified Silla, 8th century CE
L. 20.0 cm

Donggung Palace and Wolji Pond

According to *Samguk sagi*, King Munmu had a pond dug within the palace grounds in 674, around which a small hill was erected, plants and flowers were cultivated, and exotic birds and strange beasts were raised. Excavations conducted in the area of Wolji Pond in 1975 and 1976 uncovered artifacts bearing the words "*donggung*" and "*taeja*," suggesting that Donggung Palace had been located there. Also found were roof tiles and bricks inscribed with "儀鳳四年" ("*uibongsanyeon*") and "調露二年" ("*joroyinyeon*"), era years corresponding to 679 and 680, respectively, which are consistent with the record that the palace was constructed in 679.

Based on this evidence, the group of buildings to the west of Wolji Pond was originally considered to be the center of Donggung Palace, the area associated with the crown prince. In recent years, however, further research into the layout and other characteristics of this area has indicated that it was more likely used by the king, and probably included the Royal Audience Hall. The sites of Donggung Palace and Wolji Pond have yielded a variety of sophisticated artifacts not found at other locations, including roof tiles with ornate designs, Buddhist plaques, scissors used for trimming candle wicks, and decorative dragon and phoenix ornaments. Seemingly representing the advanced culture of the Silla royal court, such items strongly suggest that the area of Wolji Pond was once part of the palace grounds.

255
Padlock with Inscription: "東宮衙鎰"
Donggung Palace and Wolji Pond, Gyeongju
Unified Silla, 8th-9th century CE
L. 32.3 cm

256
Wooden Slip with Inscription: "奉太子君"
Donggung Palace and Wolji Pond, Gyeongju
Unified Silla, 8th-9th century CE
L. 6.1 cm

Excavations from the Donggung Palace and Wolji Pond area uncovered a lock bearing the inscription "東宮衙鎰" ("*donggungah il*") and a wooden slip inscribed with "奉太子君" ("*bong taejagun*"). "*Donggungah il*" means a "lock used by Donggung-ah," which was a government office believed to have overseen all affairs related to Donggung Palace, while "*bong taejagun*" refers to the crown prince ("*taeja*"). Thus, these two artifacts serve as important evidence for locating Donggung Palace near Wolji Pond.

Donggung Palace and Wolji Pond, Gyeongju

257

Brick with Inscription: "調露二年"

Donggung Palace and
Wolji Pond, Gyeongju
Unified Silla, 680 CE
W. 32.3 cm

This brick is adorned with an extravagant design of a lotus flower surrounded by ornate petals, with additional floral decorations in all four corners. One of the sides features a scene of two deer facing each other, framed by an elaborate arabesque pattern, enhancing the overall aesthetic. Another side bears an inscription reading: "Made on the third day of the third month of the second year of the Tialou era (調露, i.e., 680) by Gunyak (君若, a person's name) of Hanjibeolbu (one of Silla's six administrative divisions), belonging to the rank of *sosa* (小舍, thirteenth of seventeen ranks)."
Previously, this floral pattern and the motif of two deer were estimated to date to the mid-eighth century, but the inscription on this brick shows that those designs were in use as early as 680.

258
Jar with Lid

Donggung Palace and Wolji Pond, Gyeongju
Unified Silla, 7th century CE
H. 15.7 cm (jar)

259
Kaiyuan Tongbao Coins

Donggung Palace and Wolji Pond, Gyeongju
Unified Silla, 7th century CE
D. 2.5 cm (bottom)

Excavations at the site of a building west of Wolji Pond unearthed a lidded jar containing Kaiyuan Tongbao coins, which was likely placed in the foundation of the building prior to construction as a ritual offering to ward off evil spirits. Kaiyuan Tongbao coins began to be minted in China's Tang Dynasty in 621 and remained in circulation for nearly 300 years. According to *Samguk sagi*, Wolji was created in 674 and Donggung Palace was built in 679. These dates are supported by roof tiles and bricks excavated from the sites of Donggung Palace and Wolji Pond, which bear inscriptions of era years corresponding to 679 and 680. Thus, this jar and its coins were likely used in a ritual that took place between 674 and 680.

260
Roof-end Tiles

Donggung Palace and Wolji Pond, Gyeongju
Unified Silla, 7th century CE
D. 12.5 cm (convex roof-end tile)

This convex roof-end tile featuring a lotus design with a double layer of petals was used in conjunction with concave roof-end tiles with no upper ridge, which were decorated with arabesque patterns. This is the earliest known example of a set of roof tiles for Silla wooden buildings that features both convex and concave tiles with decorations. Recent excavations at Wolseong have confirmed that these two specific types of tiles were paired as a set.

261
Tile with Lotus Design and Green Glaze

Donggung Palace and Wolji Pond, Gyeongju
Unified Silla, 7th century CE
D. 12.9 cm

Back

Some of the convex roof-end tiles from Donggung Palace and Wolji Pond featuring a double-layered lotus were found to have been coated with a green glaze. In addition, several of the round decorative panels showed no traces of having been attached to a convex roof tile, but instead featured round or cylindrical protrusions that appear to have been used for insertion. This suggests that some of these round panels were used to decorate indoor structures, such as canopies or Buddhist altars, rather than being attached to roof tiles.

262

Roof Tile with Beast Design and Green Glaze

Donggung Palace and Wolji Pond, Gyeongju
Unified Silla, late 7th century CE
H. 29.2 cm

This decorative tile carved with the face of a beast or dragon was placed on the eaves or at the end of a descending roof. The beast face resonates with vitality, with horns and an orb on the forehead, bulging eyes, a wide gaping mouth with sharp fangs, and cloud patterns around the mouth, all rendered in a three-dimensional style. Such tiles were used to ward off evil spirits, ghosts, or other malevolent forces. To date, green-glazed roof tiles with designs of such beasts have only been excavated from Donggung Palace, Wolji Pond, Wolseong Fortress, and Sacheonwangsa Temple, suggesting a close association with the palace or royal family.

263
Roof-end Tile with Lotus Design
Donggung Palace and Wolji Pond, Gyeongju
Unified Silla, 7th century CE
D. 14.0 cm

264
Roof-end Tile with Lotus and Floral Medallion Design
Donggung Palace and Wolji Pond, Gyeongju
Unified Silla, 7th century CE
D. 15.0 cm

265
Roof-end Tile with Lotus and Floral Medallion Design
Donggung Palace and Wolji Pond, Gyeongju
Unified Silla, 7th century CE
D. 13.8 cm

266
Roof-end Tile with Honeysuckle and Floral Medallion Design
Donggung Palace and Wolji Pond, Gyeongju
Unified Silla, 7th century CE
D. 14.5 cm

267
Roof-end Tile with Lotus Design
Donggung Palace and Wolji Pond, Gyeongju
Unified Silla, 8th century CE
D. 12.8 cm

268
Roof-end Tile with Lotus Design
Donggung Palace and Wolji Pond, Gyeongju
Unified Silla, 8th century CE
D. 12.0 cm

More than 24,000 roof tiles, encompassing a wide range of types, have been excavated from Donggung Palace and Wolji Pond. In addition to their practical function of preventing rainwater and moisture from seeping into the roof, such tiles also served to embellish the appearance of a building, as evidenced by the diverse decorative patterns seen on roof-end tiles placed along the eaves. The elaborate designs of convex roof-end tiles excavated from Donggung Palace and Wolji Pond offer a glimpse into the grandeur and resplendence of the Silla palace.

269
Roof-end Tile with Lotus Design
Donggung Palace and Wolji Pond, Gyeongju
Unified Silla, 8th century CE
D. 14.0 cm

270
Roof-end Tile with Floral Medallion Design
Donggung Palace and Wolji Pond, Gyeongju
Unified Silla, 8th century CE
D. 15.4 cm

271
Roof-end Tile with Floral Medallion Design
Donggung Palace and Wolji Pond, Gyeongju
Unified Silla, 8th century CE
D. 11.0 cm

272
Roof-end Tile with Lotus and Arabesque Design
Donggung Palace and Wolji Pond, Gyeongju
Unified Silla, 9th-10th century CE
D. 13.0 cm

273
Bricks

Donggung Palace and Wolji Pond, Gyeongju
Unified Silla, late 7th-8th century CE
L. 32.0 cm (front)

274

Door Handle with Floral Medallion Design

Donggung Palace and Wolji Pond, Gyeongju
Unified Silla, 8th-9th century CE
Handle D. 13.5 cm

Excavations from Donggung Palace and Wolji Pond have yielded a variety of ornate gilt-bronze door handles. Some are decorated with an openwork floral pattern surrounded by a band of dots, while others are sculpted with the face of a fearsome beast. Those with the beast design were cast from a single mold and then gilded, with rings resembling prayer beads attached to the mouth, allowing the door to be easily opened or closed. Judging by their size, the handles with an openwork floral design seem to have been used on larger doors, while those with the faces of beasts were likely installed on smaller ones.

275

Door Handles with Bestial Face Design

Donggung Palace and Wolji Pond, Gyeongju
Unified Silla, 8th-9th century CE
L. 10.4 cm (left)

276
Lotus Bud Ornaments

Donggung Palace and Wolji Pond, Gyeongju
Unified Silla, late 7th-9th century CE
H. 18.8 cm (right)

These gilt-bronze lotus bud ornaments were likely attached to the tops of round balusters on wooden staircases, paired with a base with an openwork floral design. The lotus bud ornament on the left was secured to the baluster by a long, nail-like extension extending from beneath the base, while the one on the right seems to have been fastened with nails inserted through holes along the edge of its base.

277
End Ornament with Arabesque Design

Donggung Palace and Wolji Pond, Gyeongju
Unified Silla, late 7th-9th century CE
D. 8.1 cm

278
End Ornament with Arabesque Design

Donggung Palace and Wolji Pond, Gyeongju
Unified Silla, late 7th-9th century CE
W. 17.3 cm

Based on its size, this gilt-bronze ornament is believed to have once decorated the end of a balustrade rail. Both round and square ornaments of this type have been excavated at Donggung Palace and Wolji Pond. The ends of the railings would first be covered with a gilt bronze plate, followed by a more decorative openwork plate. Notably, slightly larger but otherwise similar openwork ornaments can be seen decorating the ends of rafters and angled rafters on a five-story pagoda from the Heijo-kyo site and in the Great Hall of Heijo Palace in Japan. Thus, it is estimated that the rafters at Donggung Palace and Wolji Pond were also finished with such openwork end decorations. This hypothesis is supported by the absence of rafter tiles at Donggung Palace and Wolji Pond, in contrast to Sacheonwangsa Temple, which was built around the same time and had rafters finished with roof tiles.

279
Wind Chime

Donggung Palace and Wolji Pond, Gyeongju
Unified Silla, late 7th-9th century CE
H. 16.0 cm

This gilt-bronze wind chime would have hung from the end of an angled rafter on a wooden building. Although it was flattened when it was discovered, it was likely round in its original form. The outer surface is evenly divided into three sections by two sets of parallel lines, with an incised arabesque pattern in each section, carved with a sharp tool. There are holes in both the top and bottom of the chime. The holes at the top were likely once used to attach a chain or cord of some type, by which the chime was hung from the roof.

280

Window Shade Ornaments

Donggung Palace and Wolji Pond, Gyeongju
Unified Silla, late 7th-9th century CE
L. 18.0-20.2 cm

These gilt-bronze ornaments were used to hold rolled-up window shades that could be unfurled to cover windows, blocking the sunlight. Each one has a ring on the top and a small lotus bud on the other end. Along with decorative wall hooks, these ornaments provide important information about the interior decoration of palaces of Unified Silla.

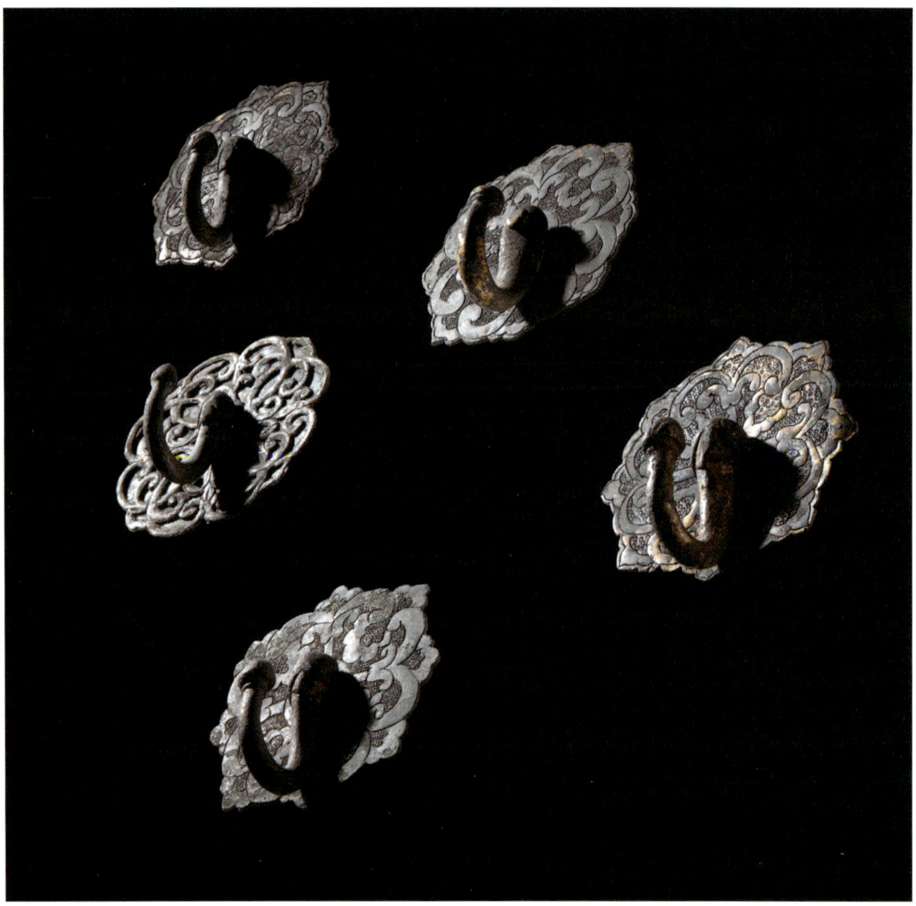

281

Decorative Wall Hooks

Donggung Palace and Wolji Pond, Gyeongju
Unified Silla, late 7th-9th century CE
L. 8.3-8.5 cm

Each of these wall hooks is attached to a decorative base adorned with embossed or engraved arabesque patterns or floral designs. Based on their form, these hooks were likely used to hang clothing or hold window shades or banners.

282
Dragon Head Decoration

Donggung Palace and Wolji Pond, Gyeongju
Unified Silla, 8th-9th century CE
L. 16.4 cm

The horns of this dragon head were cast separately and then attached. The back of the head is hollow and there are holes below the ears where nails could be affixed. The dragon headshaped ornament was previously thought to be an armrest decoration, but this is unlikely given that the nail heads are positioned on the inner side. As symbols of imperial power, ornaments shaped like dragons is closely associated with the king.

283
Phoenix-shaped Decoration

Donggung Palace and Wolji Pond, Gyeongju
Unified Silla, 8th-9th century CE
H. 10.6 cm

The body and two wings of this phoenix were all cast separately and then assembled. There are two horns sweeping backwards atop the head, scales carved into the chest, and a ring in the beak, from which decorations could be hung. Traces of gilding remain on the wings, and the feet rest on a rounded base with a protrusion at the bottom, indicating that it was once attached to another piece. Along with dragons, the phoenix was a motif specifically associated with the king or emperor, which supports the belief that the buildings around Wolji Pond were part of the royal place. The phoenix motif remained in use as a royal symbol for many generations, including in the Royal Audience Hall of palaces of the Joseon Dynasty.

Special Nature of Court Life

After unification, the Silla palace complex expanded beyond Wolseong Fortress to the east, encompassing the grounds of Donggung Palace and the area east of Wolji Pond. Excavations at various sites within this area have yielded a multitude of cultural artifacts that have shed new light on different aspects of palace life. At sites of Donggung Palace and Wolji Pond, for example, numerous metal or wood containers that were coated with lacquer were unearthed, representing the largest assemblage of such containers ever found at a single site dating to the Unified Silla period.

Other notable items include earthenware vessels, highlighted by large jars, which have rarely been found at other sites in the capital. Various implements and accessories related to daily life have also been discovered, including combs, hairpins, and rings that reveal how residents of the palace groomed and adorned themselves. All of these findings demonstrate the opulence and comfort enjoyed by members of the royal court, underscoring the wide disparity between life in the palace and life in ordinary households.

284
Juryeonggu

Donggung Palace and Wolji Pond, Gyeongju
Unified Silla, late 7th-9th century CE
H. 4.8 cm
Replica

This fourteen-sided die carved from oak wood was excavated near the stone wall on the western side of Wolji Pond. It was likely used for entertainment during court banquets, as each side contains an instruction that the person who rolled the die presumably had to follow. Many of the commands are related to alcohol, such as “Drink an entire cup of liquor and laugh loudly” and “Drink three cups of liquor at once.” These exuberant instructions evoke scenes from the lively and spirited court banquets of the time.

285
Boat

Donggung Palace and Wolji Pond, Gyeongju
Unified Silla, late 7th-9th century CE
L. 620.0 cm

This boat was constructed from three carved pieces of pinewood, with a pair of oak planks extended across the interior, one at the front and one at the rear. It is the oldest extant Silla boat, and its structure represents a developmental stage between dugout canoes and boats built with full planks of wood.

286
Bowls

Donggung Palace and Wolji Pond, Gyeongju
Unified Silla, late 7th-9th century CE
D. 15.1 cm (top left)

A number of metal dishes, plates, spoons, ladles, and other everyday utensils were excavated from Donggung Palace and Wolji Pond in Gyeongju. Very few metal utensils from the Unified Silla period have been found, giving these artifacts special significance.

287

Bowl with Lid

Donggung Palace and Wolji Pond, Gyeongju
Unified Silla, late 7th-9th century CE
H. 11.2 cm

The lid of this bowl features a jewel-shaped knob, and the character "仇" is engraved on the interior side of the cover.

288

Dishes

Donggung Palace and Wolji Pond, Gyeongju
Unified Silla, late 7th-9th century CE
D. 19.7 cm (upper left)

289
Spoons

Donggung Palace and Wolji Pond, Gyeongju
Unified Silla, 8th-9th century CE
L. 26.7 cm (far right)

290
Ladles

Donggung Palace and Wolji Pond, Gyeongju
Unified Silla, 8th-9th century CE
L. 23.0 cm (far left)

291
Lacquerware Vessels

Donggung Palace and Wolji Pond, Gyeongju
Unified Silla, 8th-9th century CE
H. 4.7 cm (left)

The excavations at Donggung Palace and Wolji Pond in Gyeongju uncovered these lacquered wooden bowls, the likes of which have rarely been found at Unified Silla sites. These bowls were first carved from wood, then covered with hemp cloth and coated with multiple layers of lacquer. Most of them were made from pinewood, although basswood was occasionally used. Some of the bowls are inscribed with one or two Chinese characters, either carved with a sharp tool or painted with vermilion lacquer.

292
Lacquerware Vessels

Donggung Palace and Wolji Pond, Gyeongju
Unified Silla, 8th-9th century CE
H. 6.1 cm (left)

293
Portable Hearth

Donggung Palace and Wolji Pond, Gyeongju
Unified Silla, 8th-9th century CE
H. 19.5 cm

This item is a portable hearth consisting of a firebox and chimney. It has two holes in the top, allowing two types of food to be cooked simultaneously. To improve fuel efficiency, a clay band was added around the opening of the firebox. Scorch marks remain visible on the inside of the hearth, confirming its use. A repeating pattern of birds in flight with outstretched wings encircles the top of the firebox, while the center is decorated with rows of dots.

294
Steamer

Donggung Palace and Wolji Pond, Gyeongju
Unified Silla, 8th-9th century CE
H. 32.8 cm

295

Bowl with Ink-painted Designs

Donggung Palace and Wolji Pond, Gyeongju
Unified Silla, 8th-9th century CE
D. 11.3 cm

Cloud designs, flower designs, and various characters are drawn on the face of the bowl. The characters "*eon*" (言), "*jeong*" (貞), and "*yeong*" (榮) were made large, while "*ta*" (唾), and "*o*" (汚) were made small. In the past, it was thought to be a tea bowl as the character "*yeong*" (榮) had been misread as "*da*" (茶). However, the repeated inscriptions of "*tao*" (唾汚) suggest that it might have been a spit bowl, or "*taho*" (唾壺).

296

Bowl with a Human Face Motif

Donggung Palace and
Wolji Pond, Gyeongju
Unified Silla, 8th-9th century CE
H. 4.9 cm

297
Lids with Stamped Design

Donggung Palace and Wolji Pond, Gyeongju
Unified Silla, 8th-9th century CE
H. 5.5 cm (left bottom)

298
Bottles with Stamped Design

Donggung Palace and Wolji Pond, Gyeongju
Unified Silla, 8th-9th century CE
H. 11.0 cm (right)

299
Bottle with Stamped Design

Donggung Palace and Wolji Pond, Gyeongju
Unified Silla, 8th-9th century CE
H. 15.5 cm

300
Pottery with Stamped Design

Donggung Palace and Wolji Pond, Gyeongju
Unified Silla, 8th-9th century CE
H. 36.3 cm (right)

Detail

301
Pottery Vessels

Donggung Palace and Wolji Pond, Gyeongju
Unified Silla, 9th-10th century CE
H. 87.7 cm (right)

Based on their size, these large jars were likely used for food storage or similar purposes. Their long necks are decorated with rough lines or wavy patterns, a characteristic decorative detail of the late Unified Silla period, when stamped patterns had disappeared.

302

Comb

Donggung Palace and Wolji Pond, Gyeongju
Unified Silla, 8th-9th century CE
L. 9.7 cm

303

Hair Part Tools

Donggung Palace and Wolji Pond, Gyeongju
Unified Silla, 8th-9th century CE
L. 14.5 cm (left)

Combs, hairpins, and glass beads were excavated at Donggung Palace and Wolji Pond in Gyeongju. Unlike similar artifacts recovered from royal tombs, which primarily consist of grave goods, these items were actually used in daily life, and thus serve as important resources for understanding court life during the Unified Silla period.

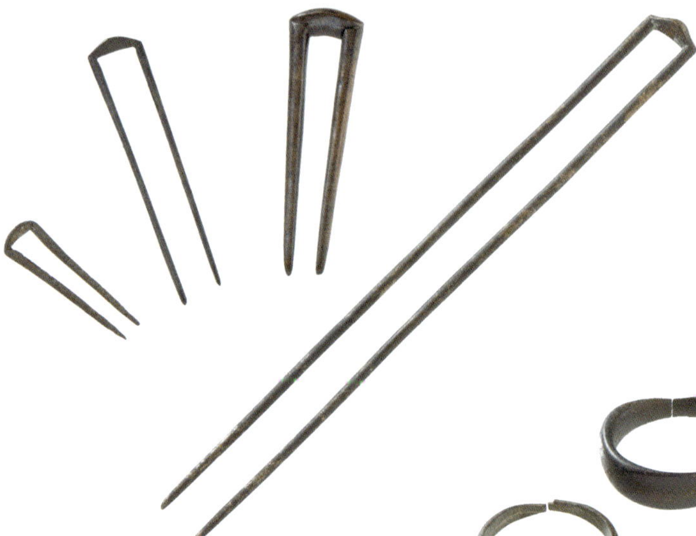

304

Hairpins

Donggung Palace and Wolji Pond, Gyeongju
Unified Silla, 8th-9th century CE
L. 9.0 cm (far right)

305

Rings

Donggung Palace and Wolji Pond, Gyeongju
Unified Silla, 8th-9th century CE
D. 2.0 cm (right)

306

Hairpin

Donggung Palace and Wolji Pond, Gyeongju
Unified Silla, 8th-9th century CE
L. 15.6 cm

307
Gold Ornaments

Donggung Palace and Wolji Pond, Gyeongju
Unified Silla, 8th-9th century CE
L. 4.5 cm (nail)

These are the only gold artifacts ever discovered at the sites of Donggung Palace and Wolji Pond in Gyeongju. The assemblage consists of one oval-shaped gold ring, four gold floral medallions, and one gold nail. Two of the floral medallions are connected by a thin gold band, while the other two each feature a single central rivet. It is likely that all four originally had gold rivets, although their exact function remains unknown.

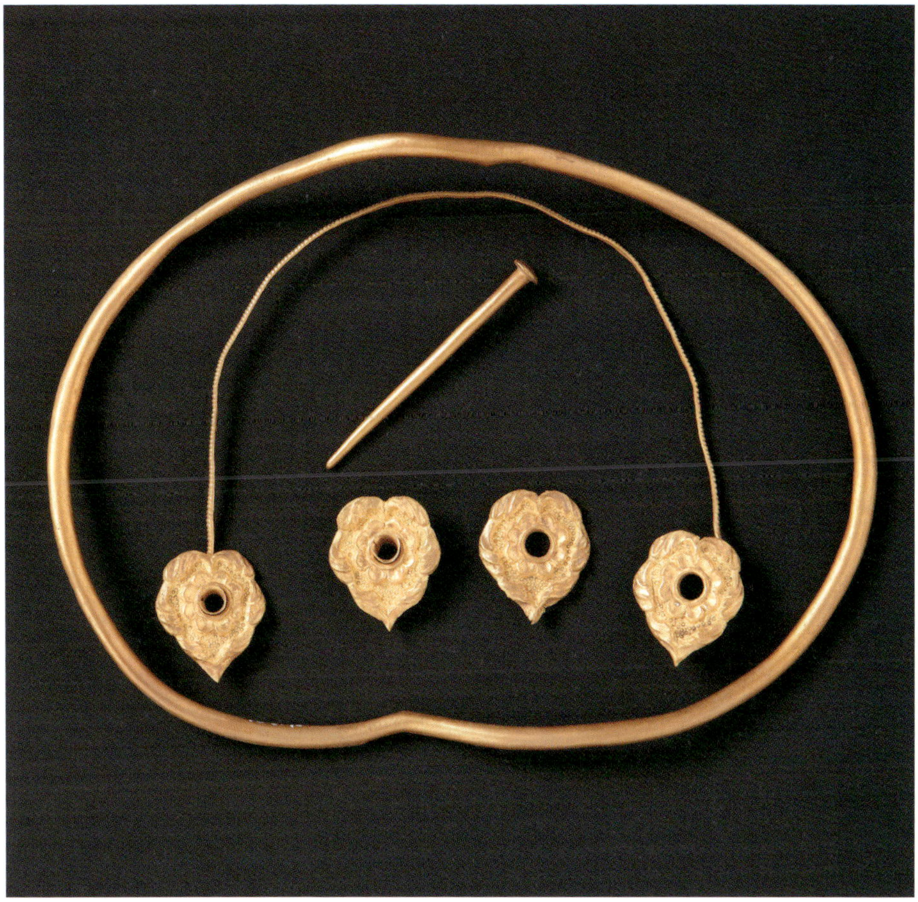

308
Glass Beads

Donggung Palace and Wolji Pond, Gyeongju
Unified Silla, 8th-9th century CE
D. 0.7-4.7 cm

Royal Tombs

The style of Silla royal tombs changed from the sixth century onward, with the large wooden chamber tombs with stone mounds being replaced by stone chamber tombs. To construct the stone chamber tombs, worked stones were stacked to form four walls, which were then topped by a ceiling stone. Notably, one of the walls had a door connecting to a passageway. This doorway enabled re-entry, allowing for multiple burials in the same tomb, which distinguished these tombs from their predecessors.

After unification in the seventh century, the royal tombs of Unified Silla continued to follow the same basic composition as tombs from the sixth century. However, after unification, each royal tomb had its own independent burial ground, as opposed to earlier royal tombs, which had often shared grounds with the tombs of aristocratic families. Royal tombs were further differentiated from ordinary tombs by the presence of stonework objects around the mound. Initially, perimeter stones and railing stones were installed to prevent the loss of soil around the tomb mound. Over time, these surrounding stones were embellished with the designs or shapes of the zodiac figures, protectors of the cardinal directions. Other stonework objects appeared around tombs of the eighth century or later, including altar stones for rituals, standing statues of civil officials, stone lion statues, and stone pillars.

In 502, when sacrificial burials were banned, *toyong* figures came to be placed within stone chamber tombs. Surviving examples of these *toyong* figures demonstrate how Silla people adopted the overall style of dress from the Tang Dynasty. Male *toyong* figures depict officials, soldiers, and servants, while female *toyong* figures depict aristocratic wives and maids.

Tomb of king Heungdeok

309
Clay Figures

Yonggang-dong, Gyeongju
Unified Silla, 8th century CE
H. 14.0 cm (front left)

During the Three Kingdoms period, it was common practice for living people to be entombed, either forcibly or voluntarily, with deceased members of royalty or aristocracy. Several such cases of sacrificial burials have been identified in stone chamber tombs with stone mounds where royals or aristocrats were buried. In 502 (third year of King Jijeung), however, sacrificial burials were banned, and *toyong* figures began to be placed in tombs instead. In the stone chamber tombs of Yonggang-dong and Hwangseong-dong in Gyeongju, both male and female *toyong* figures have been excavated. The male figures from the Hwangseong-dong tomb are dressed in Tang Dynasty-style garments, while the female figures wear traditional Silla clothing, offering fascinating insights into the clothing culture of the time.

310
Female Clay Figurine

Hwangseong-dong,
Gyeongju
Silla, 7th century CE
H. 16.5 cm

311
Male Clay Figurine

Yonggang-dong,
Gyeongju
Unified Silla, 8th century CE
H. 17.4 cm

312
Zodiac Figure (Monkey)

Tomb of King Seongdeok,
Joyang-dong, Gyeongju
Unified Silla, 8th century CE
H. 116.0 cm

Rear

313

Zodiac Figures

Hwagok-ri, Goryeong

Unified Silla, 9th century CE

H. 12.0-15.0 cm

314
Soapstone Zodiac Figures

Tomb Attributed to King Minae Mangseong-ri, Gyeongju
Unified Silla, 8th-9th century CE
H. 8.0-11.1 cm

This set of zodiac figures was discovered during renovations around the tomb believed to belong to King Minae, located in Mangseong-ri, Gyeongju. Interestingly, while zodiac figures are usually depicted standing, these soapstone figures are seated, dressed in plain clothing, with their hands held together. The carvings are relatively simple, but the head of each figure shows the distinctive features of its respective zodiac animal.

Mouse

Sheep

Rooster

Pig

315

Zodiac Figures

Temple Site in Hagu-ri, Gyeongju
Unified Silla, 9th-10th century CE
H. 42.0-45.0 cm

316

Zodiac Figures

Gyeongju · Provenance Unknown
Unified Silla
H. 106.0 cm (left)

317
Four Heavenly Kings
Gyeongju
Unified Silla
H. 95.0 cm (right)

318
Stone Door Inscribed with Guardian Deity Figure
Stone-chamber Tomb in Seoak-dong, Gyoengju
Unified Silla
H. 150.0 cm

This stone door, excavated from a stone chamber tomb in Seoak-dong, Gyeongju, features an embossed image of a guardian deity on both the front and back. The deity, whose head is encircled by a large round nimbus, wears a jeweled crown and a decorative headband with ribbons blowing upward. The upper torso is bare, while the lower body is dressed in a military uniform. The ends of a skirt are draped over both arms, with bracelets on both wrists and a long *vajra* in the right hand. The figure stands on a lotus pedestal with legs splayed symmetrically to the left and right, each adorned with anklets. The sharp eyes, hawk-like nose, and long beard convey the powerful presence of the guardian deity.

319
Stone Lion

Gyo-dong, Gyeongju
Unified Silla
H. 65.0 cm

320
Stone Lion

Provenance Unknown
Unified Silla
H. 98.0 cm

Rise of Cremation

As the entire society of Silla became increasingly devoted to Buddhism, the practice of cremation became more prevalent. The earliest known record of cremation in Silla dates to the mid-seventh century, describing how the cremated remains of the Great Monk Jajang were collected and placed in a cave. Cremation became more widespread starting in the late seventh century, after King Munmu (r. 661–681) decreed that he be cremated after his death. As this practice became more common, various types of urns were produced to hold cremated remains.

Early cremation urns consisted of pottery vessels used in everyday life or pottery with minimal decoration. Over time, the urns gradually increased in size, rings were added to secure the lid to the body, and the surfaces were decorated with more elaborate designs. But then in later periods, plain cremation urns became the norm. While most Silla cremation urns were shaped like ordinary jars, some take the form of houses or pagodas. In some cases, urns made from tri-colored glazed ware or celadon of the Tang Dynasty were put into granite stone caskets and buried.

Some Silla cremation urns consist solely of a single vessel, but others consist of two nested vessels. In such cases, the actual remains were held in the inner vessel, which was then placed into a second vessel, such as a stone coffin, stone casket, earthenware jar, or simply a hole carved into an unworked stone, for added protection. Such double urns have mostly been found in the capital area, and sometimes include vessels with elaborate stamped designs or lead-glazed ware, suggesting that they were primarily used by members of the upper class.

321
Cremation Urn with Inscription: "元和十年"
Tomb Attributed to King Minae Mangseong-ri, Gyeongju
Unified Silla, 815 CE
H. 19.3 cm

Detail

This cremation urn was discovered at the tomb formerly believed to be occupied by King Minae (r. 838–839). However, the lid bears an inscription reading "元和十年," which refers to the "tenth year of the Yuanhe era," which corresponds to the year 815. In addition, the character "井" is inscribed at the junction of the lid and the jar. This inscription casts doubt on the belief that the occupant of the tomb is King Minae, who did not die until 839.

322

Green-glazed Cremation Urns

Namsan Mountain, Gyeongju
Unified Silla, Estimated 8th century CE
H. 39.0 cm (left)

This pair of cremation urns consists of a large outer jar that held a small inner jar, where the actual cremated remains were contained. Both jars are coated with green glaze on both the inside and outside, and their exterior surfaces are filled with stamped patterns of flowers and leaves. The large outer jar features four knobs shaped like animal faces, which are evenly spaced around the shoulder, likely intended to ward off of evil spirits. Based on its lavish details, this urn was probably used for a wealthy member of the Silla aristocracy.

323
House-shaped Cremation Urn

Bukgun-dong, Gyeongju
Unified Silla, 8th century CE
H. 43.4 cm

This cremation urn is shaped like a house with a tiled roof, perhaps symbolizing the hope of providing a comfortable resting place for the spirit of the deceased. The home appears to be a stately residence, with a hipped gable roof adorned with concave and convex roof-end tiles. The outer walls are decorated with various stamped patterns, including hexagonal and floral motifs, as well as a finely incised tree, possibly representing an adjacent garden. The door and the small cremation urn that would have been placed inside the house were not found. This urn provides valuable information about the architecture of tiled-roof houses during the Unified Silla period.

324
Cremation Urn and Lid
Seokjang-dong, Gyeongju
Unified Silla
H. 23.5 cm

325
Cremation Urn with Lid
Nawon-ri, Gyeongju
Unified Silla
H. 13.8 cm

326
Cremation Urns
Gyeongju region
Unified Silla, 8th-10th century CE
H. 27.0 cm (back row, far right)

Diverse Cultures, Exchange, and Coexistence

In addition to the neighboring states of Goguryeo, Baekje, and Gaya, Silla also interacted with various Chinese dynasties, the kingdoms of the Japanese Archipelago, and even overseas regions in West Asia. Until the mid-fifth century, Silla maintained a close relationship with Goguryeo, which helped Silla send its first envoys to the Former Qin Dynasty (351–394) and also to defeat Baekje, Gaya, and the Wa (Japan) in conflicts. As a result, many foreign goods found at Silla sites from this period either originated in Goguryeo or were transmitted through it.

From the sixth century onward, Silla forged close ties with the Tang Dynasty, from whom it adopted various governmental and social systems and imported Confucian and Buddhist texts. In this period, Silla dispatched students, officials, scholars, and monks to the Tang Dynasty in pursuit of diplomatic and cultural advancement, even establishing a Silla enclave in Tang. The friendly relations between the two states are reflected in the more than 170 references to the Tang Dynasty found in *Samguk sagi*.

Silla's exchanges with West Asia are evidenced by foreign artifacts excavated from wooden chamber tombs with stone mounds in Gyeongju, such as glass vessels and the golden treasure sword in Gyerim-ro Tomb 14, as well as by the stone statues surrounding the tombs of King Wonseong and King Heungdeok. Silla also conducted exchange with the Wa (Japan), as shown by *hajiki* pottery and stone bracelets recovered from tombs in Wolseong-ro. Unified Silla's interactions with the Japanese during the Nara period (710–794) are confirmed by the numerous Silla artifacts now preserved in the Shosoin Repository of Todaiji Temple in Japan.

• Exchange with Goguryeo

Various items recovered from the Northern Mound of Hwangnamdaechong Tomb reveal the close relationship between Silla and Goguryeo, including gilt-bronze shoes, a silver-covered container with a "+"-shaped handle, and a flat-bottomed jar coated with yellow-green glaze. The gilt-bronze shoes have square-shaped nails in the soles, similar to those found in Goguryeo tombs in Jian, China. In contrast, another pair of gilt-bronze shoes excavated from Geumgwanchong Tomb do not have square nails, and also feature lotus flower motifs on the soles and "凸"-shaped openwork patterns, distinguishing them from their Goguryeo counterparts. Meanwhile, a mirror with a "TLV" pattern discovered in the Southern Mound of Hwangnamdaechong Tomb is believed to have been produced in the northern steppe regions after the third century, based on its square knob holes, raised bands around the edge, and embossed design covering the entire surface. Considering the international context at the time, this mirror most likely reached Silla via Goguryeo, rather than arriving directly from the north by a maritime route.

327
Gilt-bronze Shoes
North Mound of Hwangnamdaechong, Gyeongju
Silla, 5th century CE
L. 27.5 cm

328
Gilt-bronze Shoes
Geumgwanchong Tomb, Gyeongju
Silla, 5th century CE
L. 30.5 cm (top)

329
Silver Bowl with Lid
South Mound of Hwangnamdaechong Tomb, Gyeongju
Silla, 5th century CE
H. 16.8 cm

330
Lead-glazed Jar
Wolseong-ro Ga-5 Tomb, Gyeongju
Silla, 5th-6th century CE
H. 11.0 cm

331
Bronze Mirror
South Mound of Hwangnamdaechong Tomb, Gyeongju
Silla, 5th century CE
D. 15.5 cm

• Exchange with China

Silla's earliest interactions with the Northern and Southern dynasties of China were conducted through Goguryeo and Baekje. But after occupying the Han River basin in the sixth century, Silla initiated its own independent diplomatic relations with Chinese dynasties. Various Chinese artifacts have been discovered at Silla sites, including a belt ornament of the Sui Dynasty found in the Nuam-ri Tomb in Chungju and a glazed ceramic vessel from the Yonggang-dong Tomb in Gyeongju. Silla's alliance with the Tang Dynasty helped them to conquer Baekje and Goguryeo in the mid-seventh century, but shortly thereafter, Silla and Tang went to war with one another. Thus, relations between the two states were strained for several decades before being restored under King Seongdeok (r. 702–737), leading to active exchange, as evidenced by the large quantity of Chinese porcelain excavated from Donggung Palace and Wolji Pond, along with tri-colored glazed ware found in Joyang-dong.

332

Tri-colored Glazed Cremation Urn

Joyang-dong, Gyeongju
Unified Silla, 8th century CE
H. 16.5 cm

In 1972, this cremation urn was found inside a stone casket at the foot of a mountain in Joyang-dong, Gyeongju, about 200 meters south of King Seongdeok's tomb. Tri-colored glazed ware is a representative product of the Tang Dynasty, and is characterized by its striking coloration of brown, white, and either green or blue, which is the result of lead glaze fired at low temperatures. This urn was covered by a bronze plate that served as the lid, and originally had three legs shaped like animal paws, though one is now missing.

Wide-banded ring shaped Chinese-style Ceramics from Donggung Palace and Wolji Pond, Gyeongju

333

Celadon Bowl

Donggung Palace and Wolji Pond, Gyeongju
Tang Dynasty, 9th century CE
D. 16.2 cm

334
Stone Bracelet
Wolseong-ro Ga-29 Tomb, Gyeongju
Silla, 4th century CE
D. 8.3 cm

• Exchange with Wa (Japan)

Exchange between Silla and the Wa of Japan is evidenced by red pottery, which closely resembles Japanese *hajiki* ware, and a talc bracelet excavated from the Wolseong-ro Tomb in Gyeongju. Talc bracelets have been found in large quantities throughout the Japanese Archipelago. In addition, some of the gilt-bronze ornaments for adorning horses found in Hwangnamdaechong Tomb were inlaid with shells from the Japanese Archipelago. Other archaeological finds demonstrate that cultural interaction between Silla and the Wa continued after unification. For example, the Shosoin Repository in Japan houses a pair of candle wick scissors that are very similar to a pair excavated from Donggung Palace and Wolji Pond, as well as some *go* stones with floral and bird designs matching those found on deer bone decorations from Silla.

335
Harness Fittings
South Mound of Hwangnamdaechong, Gyeongju
Silla, 5th century CE
H. 4.5 cm (left)

336
Japanese *Hajiki*-style Pottery
Wolseong-ro Ga-31 Tomb, Gyeongju
Silla, 4th century CE
H. 12.6 cm (far right)

337
Candle Wick Scissors

Donggung Palace and Wolji Pond, Gyeongju
Unified Silla, 8th century CE
L. 25.5 cm
Treasure

Discovered in a layer of mud approximately 110 centimeters east of the site of Building 3, west of Wolji Pond, these gilt-bronze scissors were used for trimming candle wicks, likely in conjunction with gilt-bronze candlesticks. The two blades end in a hemispheric cup that would catch the end of the wick after it was cut. The handles are shaped like vines, and the upper side is ornately decorated with bell and arabesque patterns. A similar pair of scissors is housed in the Shosoin Repository of Todaiji Temple in Japan, suggesting active cultural exchange between Silla and the Wa.

Scissors in the Shosoin Repository

338

Deer Bone Decorations with Floral and Bird Designs

Donggung Palace and Wolji Pond, Gyeongju
Unified Silla, 8th-9th century CE
L. 21.8 cm (far right)

These decorative ornaments, which are believed to have been attached to wooden furniture, are carved from deer bones. They are finely worked on one side, with small holes drilled at regular intervals and alternating images of birds and flowers incised between the holes. This particular bird motif is thought to have originated in West Asia, perhaps around Persia, though it also appears in Chinese iconography after the Han Dynasty. Notably, similar bird motifs can be seen on *go* stones in the collection of the Shosoin Repository at Todaiji Temple in Japan, indicating cultural exchange between Silla and the Wa.

Go Stones in the Shosoin Repository

339
Glassware
North Mound of Hwangnamdaechong Tomb, Gyeongju
Silla, 5th century CE
H. 7.6 cm

From West to East

Silla also conducted international exchange with people in Siberia and West Asia. Some gold crowns and belt ornaments found in Silla royal tombs do not match any artifacts from Goguryeo, Baekje, or China, and instead appear to be associated with the Altai region in southern Siberia, where gold held particular significance. Furthermore, glass vessels, daggers with a gold scabbard, horn cups, and inlaid glass necklaces from Silla sites resemble artifacts discovered around the Mediterranean and in West Asia in both shape and craftsmanship. The golden treasure sword excavated from Gyeonglim-ro Tomb 14 in Gyeongju is strikingly similar to a sword from the Borovoye site in Kazakhstan, and is thus believed to have been produced in Central Asia, between the Black Sea and China, before being brought to Silla. Additionally, some guardian statues from the royal tombs of Unified Silla seem to depict people of foreign descent, and may have been inspired by West Asians who served in Silla. The presence of such international artifacts suggests that Silla was not merely a small kingdom in the southeastern corner of the Korean Peninsula, but a cosmopolitan state recognized as far away as West Asia.

340
Glassware
Geumgwanchong Tomb, Gyeongju
Silla, 5th century CE
H. 9.2 cm

One of the most prized foreign objects in Silla was glassware. This is demonstrated by the discovery of glass vessels in the royal tombs of Hwangnamdaechong, Seobongchong, Geumgwanchong, Geumnyeongchong, and Cheonmachong, all of which yielded gold crowns and are therefore believed to be the burials of kings or queens. The glass vessels brought to Silla were produced with the most advanced technology available at the time and are believed to have originated in Syria, along the eastern Mediterranean coast, or in Sasanian Persia. To date, twenty-five glass vessels have been excavated from Silla sites, including eleven from Hwangnam daechong Tomb (seven from the South Mound and four from the North Mound).

341
Glass Bowl
South Mound of Hwangnamdaechong Tomb, Gyeongju
Silla, 5th century CE
H. 6.7 cm

342
Glassware
North Mound of Hwangnamdaechong Tomb, Gyeongju
Silla, 5th century CE
H. 7.3 cm

343
Glassware

Cheonmachong Tomb, Gyeongju
Silla, 6th century CE
H. 7.4 cm
Treasure

344
Glass Pendant
Gyerim-ro Tomb 14, Gyeongju
Silla, 6th century CE
L. 4.9 cm

345
Harness Fittings
Gyerim-ro Tomb 14, Gyeongju
Silla, 6th century CE
L. 2.4 cm (far right)

346
Necklace with Inlaid Glass Bead
Tomb 4 of Michuwangneung Tomb District C, Gyeongju
Silla, 5th-6th century CE
L. 24.0 cm
Treasure

This inlaid glass bead, excavated from the Michuwangneung Tomb District in Hwangnam-dong, Gyeongju, is only 1.8 cm in diameter. Despite its small size, however, it features an array of motifs expressed with advanced inlay techniques, including the white faces of a man and woman who do not appear to be from Silla, with large blue eyes, high bridged noses, and faintly smiling red lips. The faces are surrounded by birds that seem to be flying in a flock and thin branches with beautiful flowers, conveying incredible splendor and sophistication. Such inlaid glass beads were originally produced along the Mediterranean coast before spreading to other regions, including West Asia, Southeast Asia, China, the Korean Peninsula, and the Japanese Archipelago.

Detail

347

Golden Treasure Sword

Gyerim-ro Tomb 14, Gyeongju
Silla, before 6th century CE
L. 36.0 cm
Treasure

This golden treasure sword was found on one of the two men interred in Gyerim-ro Tomb 14. The sword's scabbard and hilt have an unusual shape. Both are made from gold and lavishly adorned with red garnets and gold designs, including gold granules attached with a special filigree technique. Based on its resemblance to another sword that was excavated in Borovoye, Kazakhstan, this sword is believed to have been made in Central Asia and brought to Silla.

348
Drinking Horn and Stand
Tomb 7 of Michuwangneung Tomb District C, Gyeongju
Silla, 5th-6th century CE
H. 17.0 cm

349
Gilt bronze Drinking Horn
Geumgwanchong Tomb,
Gyeongju
Silla, 5th century CE
L. 23.7 cm

350
Drinking Horn
Naengsu-ri, Pohang
Silla, 6th century CE
L. 27.8 cm

351
Corner Pillar
Square Tomb in Gujeong-dong, Gyeongju
Unified Silla, 9th-10th century CE
H. 73.6 cm

352
Stone with Lion and Peacock Designs
Gyeongju
Unified Silla, 8th century CE
L. 300.0 cm

VI.

Decline of Silla and Transition to the Goryeo Dynasty

353
Portrait of King Gyeongsun
Empire of Korea, 1904 CE
Painting on Silk
152.5×87.5 cm
Collection at Sunghyejeon Shrine

After unification, the Silla Kingdom enjoyed a period of social stability and prosperity with a strong royal authority. But starting around the mid-eighth century, their political foundation began to weaken due to corruption and power struggles among the aristocracy. During the reign of King Hyegong (r. 765–780), high-ranking aristocrats rebelled multiple times, ultimately leading to the king's death and the ascension of King Seondeok. Over the next 150 years, more than twenty kings occupied the throne, and the conflicts among powerful aristocratic factions continued unabated. As a result, royal tombs from this period became smaller and much less elaborate, unadorned with the funerary monuments or grave goods seen in previous generations. Taking advantage of the weakened central government, local gentry in the provinces increasingly asserted their power, often by commissioning the construction of Buddhist temples. Also in this period, ornate funerary monuments for prominent monks became widespread.

As Silla struggled to quell its internal disorder, Gungye (d. 918) and Gyeon Hwon (867–936) founded the kingdoms of Hugoguryeo (Later Goguryeo) and Hubaekje (Later Baekje), respectively, marking the beginning of the Later Three Kingdoms period. The Silla royal family lost control over both the aristocracy and the general populace, leading to a rapid decline in its authority. Ultimately, King Gyeongsun (r. 927–935) surrendered to King Taejo of Goryeo (r. 918–943), bringing an end to the Silla Kingdom, which had flourished for nearly a thousand years.

Goryeo established itself as a more open society than Silla, politically, economically, and socially. While Goryeo maintained a rank system, it was more meritocratic than Silla, which had been dominated by the "True Bone" (*jingol*) aristocracy. In addition to Buddhism, Goryeo embraced Confucianism, Taoism, and traditional beliefs, allowing for the coexistence of various religions and ideologies. Thus, Goryeo succeeded in resolving many of Silla's political and social contradictions, laying the foundation for a new dynastic order.

354

Bottle with Flattened Sides and Bottles with Incised Line Pattern

Cheonghaejin, Wando
Unified Silla
H. 32.7 cm (left)

Jang Bogo (d. 846) was born and raised in the provinces of Silla. In the early ninth century, he traveled to the Tang Dynasty and became a general in the Wuning Defense Command of Xuzhou, where he excelled in martial arts. He returned home in 828 (third year of King Heungdeok), where he was awarded the rank of *daesa* and ordered to build Cheonghaejin Fort at Wando, a strategic hub for maritime transportation. From Cheonghaejin, with 10,000 troops under his command, Jang Bogo protected sea trade routes, eradicated piracy, and steadily increased his stature by controlling maritime traffic and engaging in international trade. He also intervened in disputes about royal succession, aiding in the ascension of King Sinmu (r. 839). He later arranged for his daughter to marry King Munseong (r. 839–857), but the marriage was called off due to opposition from court officials. In 846, Jang Bogo led an unsuccessful rebellion, in which he was killed. As a result, Cheonghaejin Fort was destroyed and its residents were relocated to Byeokgol-gun (present-day Gimje). These three bottles are among various items that have been recovered from the former site of Cheonghaejin.

355

Portrait of Choi Chiwon

Joseon, 1793 CE
Painting on Silk
140.0×100.0 cm
Collection of the Gyeongju Choi Clan

Choi Chiwon (b. 857) was a renowned literary figure, government official, and Confucian scholar active during the final years of the Unified Silla period. Born into the *yukdupum* rank, he traveled to the Tang Dynasty to study and successfully passed the "Bingongke," a civil service examination for foreigners. He served as a sub-prefect and administrative officer in Lishui County, and is especially noted for his work *Tohwangsogyeongmun* (*Address to Huang Chao*), written during the Huang Chao Rebellion. Upon returning to Silla, Choi Chiwon composed eulogies for eminent monks, wrote diplomatic documents, and sought to reform the declining state through measures and principles he had learned in China. In 894, he submitted a proposal to Queen Jinsung containing ten reform measures, but they were never implemented. Disillusioned, he withdrew from public life and entered seclusion.

Temples in Gyeongju during the Goryeo Dynasty

After the fall of Silla, all of the country's major government institutions, information systems, and technological infrastructure were relocated from Gyeongju to Gaegyeong, the new capital of the Goryeo Dynasty. But even after this shift in political power and Gyeongju's relegation to a regional city, the royal lineage and local population still strived to preserve the history and cultural heritage of Silla.
The Buddhist culture of the late Unified Silla period persisted into the Goryeo era, with Hwangnyongsa Temple continuing to serve as a spiritual center. The temple received support from the Goryeo royal family and aristocracy and was renovated several times before being destroyed during the Mongol invasions in 1238. Records also show that Cheonryongsa Temple in Gyeongju was rebuilt and Seokgatap Pagoda at Bulguksa Temple was restored during the Goryeo period. The continued significance of local temples is also supported by inscriptions on Goryeo bronze gongs excavated at the sites of Gulbulsa and Gameunsa Temples, and the discovery of various Goryeo artifacts, including roof tiles, bowls, and Buddhist offerings, at the temple sites of Gulbulsa, Gameunsa, and Mangdeoksa. Furthermore, some Goryeo-era roof tiles found in Gyeongju are inscribed with the names of temples that are absent from historical texts, such as Gabsansa and Sajesa, affirming that a number of temples in Gyeongju remained active throughout the Goryeo Dynasty.

356
Sarira Reliquaries (Sarira Bottle, Sarira Casket, Rings, Beads)
Three-story Stone Pagoda at the Seungansa Temple Site, Hamyang
Goryeo, 10th century CE
D. 8.5 cm (sarira casket)

During the process of moving a three-story stone pagoda from the Seungansa Temple site in Hamyang-gun, these sarira reliquary items were discovered in a chamber carved into the body stone of the pagoda's first-story. The cylindrical bronze sarira casket held a green glass sarira bottle containing one sarira, a string of glass beads, and seven rings made of silver and nickel. Other miscellaneous items discovered in the chamber include a piece of silk and a pouch that contained a piece of paper with a message written in ink, which stated that the pagoda was rebuilt in 1494 (twenty-fifth year of Joseon's King Seongjong).

• Bronze Gong

An inscription along the side of this bronze gong states that it was made in 1183 through the prayers of Lee Baekyu, a former community leader. Two rings are attached to the top of the gong, which were used to hang it. The area where the gong was struck is decorated with a central design of a lotus seed pod surrounded by lotus, as well as cloud and vine patterns rendered in relief.

The inscription reads: "Fourth month, twenty-third day of the *gyemyo* year, the twenty-third year of the Dading era (1183). Placed in Gulseoksa Temple on Buksan Mountain in the city of Donggyong, made from 7 *geun* (approximately 4.4 kg) of metal. The person responsible for its production was the former community leader Lee Baekyu, its production was overseen by □□, and the craftsperson was Uiseong."

357
Buddhist Ritual Offering Implements from Mangdeoksa Temple Site

Mangdeoksa Temple site, Gyeongju
Goryeo
H. 33.0 cm (vase)

大定二十三年癸卯四月 日

東京北山屈石寺排入重七斤

次知造前戶長李伯兪

棟梁道人□□大匠義成

358
Bronze Gong
Gulbulsa Temple Site, Gyeongju
Goryeo, 1183 CE
L. 33.6 cm

List of Plates

Silla History Exhibition Hall   Silla Art Exhibition Hall   Wolji Exhibition Hall   Outdoor Exhibition

001
Pick
Maae-ri, Andong
Paleolithic Period
L. 23.6 cm

002
Chopping Tools
Maae-ri, Andong
Paleolithic Period
L. 13.9 cm (left)

003
Stone Hammers
Maae-ri, Andong
Paleolithic Period
L. 14.4 cm (far left)

004
Blades, Core
Sinhwa-ri, Ulsan · Sanseo-ri, Pohang
Paleolithic Period
L. 6.7 cm (far right)
Gyeongju National Museum, Ulsan Museum

005
Refitted Stone Tools
Sinhwa-ri, Ulsan
Paleolithic Period
L. 8.4-10.8 cm (bottom left)
Ulsan Museum

006
Stone Harpoons
Jukbyeon-ri, Uljin
Neolithic Period
L. 9.9 cm (right)

007
Fishing Hooks
Jukbyeon-ri, Uljin
Neolithic Period
L. 13.0 cm (top left)

008
Stone Digging Tools
Jukbyeon-ri, Uljin
Neolithic Period
L. 20.3 cm (right)

009
Various Types of Stone Tools
Bonggil-ri, Gyeongju · Jukbyeon-ri, Uljin
Neolithic Period
L. 11.5 cm (far right)

010
Oar
Jukbyeon-ri, Uljin
Neolithic Period
L. 170.0 cm

011
Boat Fragment
Jukbyeon-ri, Uljin
Neolithic Period
W. 64.0 cm

012
Pottery
Bonggil-ri, Gyeongju · Songjuk-ri, Gimcheon · Jukbyeon-ri, Uljin
Neolithic Period
H. 42.6 cm (back row, right)

013
Comb-pattern Pottery
Songjuk-ri, Gimcheon
Neolithic Period
H. 35.0 cm

014
Ornaments
Hupo-ri, Uljin
Neolithic Period
L. 11.4 cm (far right)

015
Stone Axes
Hupo-ri, Uljin
Neolithic Period
L. 54.2 cm (far left)

016
Stone Axes
Gapsan-ri, Gyeongju · Joyang-dong, Gyeongju · Jinrali, Cheongdo
Bronze Age
L. 13.2 cm (left)

017
Stone Adzes
Seokjang-dong, Gyeongju · Sinpyeong-ri, Yeongdeok · Jinra-ri, Cheongdo
Bronze Age
L. 22.3 cm (top left)

018
Stone Sickles
Chunghyo-dong, Gyeongju · Yongjang-ri, Gyeongju · Sangan-dong, Ulsan
Bronze Age
L. 26.3 cm (top)

019
Stone Chisels
Gapsan-ri, Gyeongju · Seokjang-dong, Gyeongju
Bronze Age
L. 7.7 cm (left)

020
Various types of Stone Tools
Gyeongsang-do
Bronze Age
L. 13.8 cm (bottom right)

021
Semi-lunar Stone Knifes
Gyeongsangbuk-do
Bronze Age
L. 11.6 cm (center)

022
Red Burnished Pottery
Wolsan-ri, Gyeongju · Chunghyo-dong,
Gyeongju · Cheongdo
Bronze Age
H. 13.9 cm (center)

023
Pottery
Gyeongsangbuk-do
Bronze Age
H. 58.2 cm (back row, left)

024
Ground Stone Dagger
Gaknam-myeon, Cheongdo
Bronze Age
L. 41.0 cm

025
***Bipa*-shaped Bronze Dagger**
Yejeon-ri, Cheongdo
Bronze Age
L. 34.8 cm

026
Stone Moon Mace
Doji-dong, Gyeongju · Dongcheon-dong, Gyeongju · Hwangseong-dong, Gyeongju · Gajaegol, Ulsan · Chogok-ri, Pohang
Bronze Age
D. 10.7 cm (top right)
Gyeongju National Museum, Ulsan Museum

027
Ground Stone Daggers
Gyeongsangbuk-do
Bronze Age
L. 20.0 cm (far left)

028
Stone Arrowheads
Gyeongsangbuk-do
Bronze Age
L. 11.6 cm (botton left)

029
Slender Bronze Daggers
Gyeongsangbuk-do · Pyongyang
Early Iron Age–Proto Three Kingdoms Period
L. 31.5 cm (far right)

030
Various Types of Bronze Artifacts
Gyeongsangbuk-do · Pyongyang
Early Iron Age-Proto Three Kingdoms Period
L. 51.3 cm (bottom left)

031
Bronze Artifacts
Jukdong-ri, Gyeongju
1st century BCE
L. 23.0 cm (slender bronze dagger)
Treasure
Gift of Lee Yang-sun

032
Bronze Mirrors
Joyang-dong, Gyeongju
1st century BCE
D. 8.0 cm (right)

033
Bronze Dagger-Axe Sheath and Iron Dagger-Axe
Yongjeon-ri, Yeongcheon
1st century BCE
L. 32.0 cm

034
Bronze Crossbow Trigger Mechanism
Yongjeon-ri, Yeongcheon
1st century BCE
L. 8.3 cm

035
Various Types of Iron Artifacts
Yongjeon-ri, Yeongcheon
1st century BCE
L. 48.0 cm (top)

036
Sara-ri Tomb 130 Excavated Artifacts
Sara-ri Tomb 130, Gyeongju
1st century CE
L. 46.5 cm (lacquered scabbard for iron dagger)

037
Slender Bronze Dagger and Scabbard Fittings
Sara-ri Tomb 130, Gyeongju
1st century CE
Restoration L. 56.8 cm (bronze dagger)

038
***Wajil* Pottery**
Gyeongju
1st-4th century CE
H. 21.8 cm (front right)

039
Bird-shaped Pottery
Gyeongju
Three Kingdoms Period
H. 43.6 cm (back row, left)

040
Molds
Hwangseong-dong, Gyeongju
Silla, 3rd-4th century CE
L. 22.3 cm (far right)

041
Tuyere
Hwangseong-dong, Gyeongju
Silla, 3rd-4th century CE
L. 42.5 cm

042
Gorget and Waist Armor
Gueo-ri Tomb 1, Gyeongju
Silla, 3rd century CE
H. 22.0 cm (gorget)

043
Gueo-ri Tomb 1 Excavated Artifacts
Guero-ri Tomb 1, Gyeongju
Silla, 3rd century CE
H. 36.4 cm (vessel stand)

044
Chamfron
Sara-ri, Gyeongju
Silla, 5th century CE
L. 48.0 cm

045
Plate Armor
Gujeong-dong, Gyeongju
Silla, 4th century CE
H. 71.0 cm (including gorget)

046
Plate Armor
Dongsan-ri Tomb 34, Gyeongju
Silla, 4th century CE
H. 52.0 cm
(including gorget)

047
Plate Armor
Masan-ri, Pohang
Silla, 4th century CE
H. 69.1 cm
(including gorget)

048
Plate Armor
Sara-ri, Tomb 55, Gyeongju
Silla, 5th century CE
H. 60.5 cm (except helmet)

049
Necklaces
Gyeongju
Silla, 3rd century CE
L. 46.5 cm (far left)

050
Gold Bowls
Wolseong-ro Tomb Ga-13, Gyeongju
Silla, 4th-5th century CE
H. 5.2 cm (left)

051
Gold Dangling Pendants
Wolseong-ro Tomb Ga-13, Gyeongju
Silla, 4th-5th century CE
L. 26.4 cm (far right)

052
Gold Ornaments
Wolseong-ro Tomb Ga-13, Gyeongju
Silla, 4th-5th century CE
L. 65.3 cm (far right)

053
Gold Crown
Gyo-dong, Gyeongju
Silla, 5th century CE
H. 12.8 cm

054
Gold Crown
North Mound of Hwangnamdaechong Tomb, Gyeongju
Silla, 5th century CE
H. 27.3 cm
National Treasure

055
Gold Crown
Seobongchong Tomb, Gyeongju
Silla, 5th century CE
H. 35.0 cm
Treasure

056
Gold Crown
Geumgwanchong Tomb, Gyeongju
Silla, 5th century CE
H. 27.5 cm
National Treasure

057
Gold Crown
Geumnyeongchong Tomb, Gyeongju
Silla, 6th century CE
H. 27.0 cm
Treasure

058
Gold Crown
Cheonmachong Tomb, Gyeongju
Silla, 6th century CE
H. 32.5 cm
National Treasure

059
Gold Crown Cap
Geumgwanchong Tomb, Gyeongju
Silla, 5th century CE
H. 19.0 cm
National Treasure

060
Gold Crown Ornament
Geumgwanchong Tomb, Gyeongju
Silla, 5th century CE
H. 40.8 cm
National Treasure

061
Gold Earrings
Geumgwanchong Tomb, Gyeongju
Silla, 5th century CE
L. 8.7 cm

062
Gold Earrings
Geumgwanchong Tomb, Gyeongju
Silla, 5th century CE
L. 10.0 cm

063
Gold and Silver Ornaments
Geumgwanchong Tomb, Gyeongju
Silla, 5th century CE
L. 14.8 cm
(top right)

064
Gold Belt
Geumgwanchong Tomb, Gyeongju
Silla, 5th century CE
L. 109.0 cm
National Treasure

065
Large Sword with Ring-shaped Pommel with Inscription: "尒斯智王"
Geumgwanchong Tomb, Gyeongju
Silla, 5th century CE
L. 87.0 cm

066
Silver Crown Cap
South Mound of Hwangnamdaechong Tomb, Gyeongju
Silla, 5th century CE
H. 15.4 cm

067
Gold Crown Ornament
South Mound of Hwangnamdaechong Tomb, Gyeongju
Silla, 5th century CE
L. 59.0 cm
Treasure

068
Gilt-bronze Belt with Jewel Beetle Wings
South Mound of Hwangnamdaechong Tomb, Gyeongju
Silla, 5th century CE
L. 4.0 cm (each)

069
Gilt Bronze Shoes
South Mound of Hwangnamdaechong Tomb, Gyeongju
Silla, 5th century CE
L. 34.5 cm

070
Spindle Whorl-shaped Stone Tools
North Mound of Hwangnamdaechong Tomb, Gyeongju
Silla, 5th century CE
D. 8.1 cm

071
Silver Belt
North Mound of Hwangnamdaechong Tomb, Gyeongju
Silla, 5th century CE
L. 51.6 cm

072
Belt-end Section with Inscription: "夫人帶"
North Mound of Hwangnamdaechong Tomb, Gyeongju
Silla, 5th century CE
L. 12.3 cm

073
Swords with Ring Pommel
South Mound of Hwangnamdaechong Tomb, Gyeongju
Silla, 5th century CE
L. 32.0 cm (far left)

074
Gold and Silver Vessels
Hwangnamdaechong Tomb, Gyeongju
Silla, 5th century CE
H. 9.1. cm (back row, left)

075
Bronze Bowls with Lid
South Mound of Hwangnamdaechong Tomb, Gyeongju
Silla, 5th century CE
H. 12.0 cm (far right)

076
Bronze Cauldrons
Hwangnamdaechong Tomb, Gyeongju
Silla, 5th century CE
H. 16.8 cm (right)

077
Jars with Spout
South Mound of Hwangnamdaechong Tomb, Gyeongju
Silla, 5th century CE
L. 16.2 cm (right)

078
Ladles
South Mound of Hwangnamdaechong Tomb, Gyeongju
Silla, 5th century CE
L. 38.6 cm (top)

079
Gilt-bronze Saddlebow
South Mound of Hwangnamdaechong Tomb, Gyeongju
Silla, 5th century CE
L. 55.3 cm

080
Forearm Covers
South Mound of Hwangnamdaechong Tomb, Gyeongju
Silla, 5th century CE
H. 34.4 cm (front)

081
Stirrups
South Mound of Hwangnamdaechong Tomb, Gyeongju
Silla, 5th century CE
L. 23.0 cm (top right)

082
Harness Fittings
South Mound of Hwangnamdaechong Tomb, Gyeongju
Silla, 5th century CE
L. 4.8 cm (left)

083
Horse Trappings
South Mound of Hwangnamdaechong Tomb, Gyeongju
Silla, 5th century CE
L. 54.7 cm (top left)

084
Horse Trappings
South Mound of Hwangnamdaechong Tomb, Gyeongju
Silla, 5th century CE
L. 13.8 cm (bottom left)

085
Iron Halberds
South Mound of Hwangnamdaechong Tomb, Gyeongju
Silla, 5th century CE
L. 62.2 cm (center)

086
Gold Crown Cap
Cheonmachong Tomb, Gyeongju
Silla, 6th century CE
H. 19.0 cm
National Treasure

087
Gold Crown Ornament
Cheonmachong Tomb, Gyeongju
Silla, 6th century CE
H. 40.8 cm
Treasure

088
Gold Crown Ornament
Cheonmachong Tomb, Gyeongju
Silla, 6th century CE
H. 23.0 cm
Treasure

089
Bamboo Mudguard with Celestial Horse Painting and Gilt Bronze Ornament
Cheonmachong Tomb, Gyeongju
Silla, 6th century CE
56.0×81.0 cm

090
Birch Bark Mudguard with Celestial Horse Painting (placed above)
Cheonmachong Tomb, Gyeongju
Silla, 6th century CE
54.7×73.5 cm
National Treasure

091
Birch Bark Mudguard with Celestial Horse Painting (placed below)
Cheonmachong Tomb, Gyeongju
Silla, 6th century CE
55.2×73.2 cm
National Treasure

092
Gold Ornament
Geumgwanchong Tomb, Gyeongju
Silla, 5th century CE
L. 11.3 cm (triangle)

093
Gold Ornament
Geumgwanchong Tomb, Gyeongju
Silla, 5th century CE
L. 30.0 cm

094
Gold Earrings
Hwango-dong Tomb 5, Gyeongju
Silla, 5th-6th century CE
L. 8.5 cm

095
Gold Earrings
Cheonmachong Tomb, Gyeongju
Silla, 6th century CE
L. 6.0 cm

096
Gold Earrings
Cheonmachong Tomb, Gyeongju
Silla, 6th century CE
L. 5.0 cm

097
Gold Earrings
Hwango-dong Tomb 4, Gyeongju
Silla, 5th-6th century CE
L. 9.6 cm

098
Gold Earrings
Cheonmachong Tomb, Gyeongju
Silla, 6th century CE
L. 6.2 cm

099
Gold Earrings
Noseo-dong Tomb 138, Gyeongju
Silla, 5th-6th century CE
L. 10.5 cm

100
Gold Earrings
Gyerim-ro Tomb 14, Gyeongju
Silla, 5th-6th century CE
L. 7.0 cm

101
Gold Earrings
South Mound of Hwangnamdaechong Tomb, Gyeongju
Silla, 5th century CE
L. 5.5 cm

102
Gold Earrings
Hwango-dong Tomb 14, Gyeongju
Silla, 5th century CE
L. 6.1 cm

103
Gold Earrings
Hwangnam-dong Tomb 151, Gyeongju
Silla, 5th-6th century CE
L. 7.3 cm

104
Gold Earrings
Hwangnam-dong Tomb 82, Gyeongju
Silla, 5th-6th century CE
L. 6.9 cm

105
Gold Dangling Pendants
North Mound of Hwangnamdaechong Tomb, Gyeongju
Silla, 5th century CE
L. 19.2 cm

106
Gold Dangling Pendants
North Mound of Hwangnamdaechong Tomb, Gyeongju
Silla, 5th century CE
L. 25.9 cm

107
Gold Dangling Pendants
Hwango-dong, Gyeongju
Silla, 5th-6th century CE
L. 9.0 cm

108
Gold Dangling Pendants
Tomb 4 of Michuwangneung Tomb District C, Gyeongju
Silla, 6th century CE
L. 16.8 cm
Treasure

109
Gold Dangling Pendants
Gyo-dong, Gyeongju
Silla, 5th century CE
L. 13.0 cm

110
Gold Dangling Pendants
North Mound of Hwangnamdaechong Tomb, Gyeongju
Silla, 5th century CE
L. 18.5 cm

111
Gold Dangling Pendants
Hwango-dong, Gyeongju
Silla, 5th-6th century CE
L. 20.6 cm

112
Gold and Silver Rings
Gyeongju
Silla, 5th-6th century CE
D. 2.5 cm (bottom row, center)

113
Gold Bracelets
Indongchong Tomb, Gyeongju · Cheonmachong Tomb, Gyeongju · North Mound of Hwangnamdaechong Tomb, Gyeongju
Silla, 5th-6th century CE
D. 7.3 cm (far left)

114
Gold Necklace
South Mound of Hwangnamdaechong Tomb, Gyeongju
Silla, 5th century CE
L. 66.4 cm
National Treasure

115
Chestlace
Wolseong-ro Tomb Ga-13, Gyeongju
Silla, 4th-5th century CE
L. 43.5 cm

116
Chestlace
Cheonmachong Tomb, Gyeongju
Silla, 6th century CE
L. 63.0 cm
Treasure

117
Various Types of Pottery
South Mound of Hwangnamdaechong Tomb, Gyeongju · Goesi-ri, Yeongdeok
Silla, 5th-6th century CE
H. 10.5 cm (far left)

118
Vessel Stands and Mounted Long-necked Jars
Deokcheon-ri, Gyeongju · Inwang-dong, Gyeongju · South Mound of Hwangnamdaechong Tomb, Gyeongju · Goesi-ri, Yongdok
Silla, 5th-6th century CE
H. 43.9 cm (far left)

119
Vessel Stand and Mounted Dishes with Lid
North Mound of Hwangnamdaechong Tomb, Gyeongju
Silla, 5th century CE
H. 16.4 cm (vessel stand)

120
Vessel Stands
South Mound of Hwangnamdaechong Tomb, Gyeongju
Silla, 5th century CE
H. 53.8 cm (back)

121
Figurative Pottery
Deokcheon-ri, Gyeongju · Sara-ri, Gyeongju · Michuwangneung Tomb District, Gyeongju
Silla, 4th-6th century CE
H. 20.0 cm (far left)

122
House-shaped Pottery
Sara-ri, Gyeongju
Silla, 4th century CE
H. 20.3 cm

123
Auspicious Animal-shaped Pottery
Tomb 3 of Michuwangneung Tomb District C,
Gyeongju
Silla, 6th century CE
H. 12.5 cm
Treasure

124
Human · Animal Clay Figurines
Hwangnam-dong, Gyeongju · Provenance Unknown
Silla, 5th-6th century CE
H. 26.0 cm (back row, left)

125
Pottery with Clay Figurines
Wolseong-ro Tomb, Gyeongju · Provenance Unknown
Silla, 5th-6th century CE
H. 11.0 cm (far left)

126
Lid with Images
Gyerim-ro Tomb 47, Gyeongju
Silla, 5th century CE
D. 15.0 cm

127
Lid with Horse Images
Provenance Unknown
Silla, 5th-6th century CE
D. 21.0 cm

128
Jar with Clay Figurines
Michuwangneung Tomb District 12, Gyeongju
Silla, 5th century CE
H. 40.5 cm
National Treasure

129
Oath Stone Inscribed in the "*Imshin*" Year
Geumjang-ri, Gyeongju
Silla, 6th-7th century CE
H. 32.0 cm
Treasure

130
Jungseong-ri Stele from Pohang
Jungseong-ri, Pohang
Silla, 501 CE
H. 105.6 cm
National Treasure
Gyeongju National Research Institute of Cultural Heritage

131
Myeonghwalsanseong Fortress Stele
Bomun-dong, Gyeongju
Silla, 511 CE
H. 66.8 cm

132
Namsansinseong Fortress Stelae
Namsan Mountain, Gyeongju
Silla, 591 CE
H. 91.0 cm (Stele No. 1)

133
Stele Commemorating the Martyrdom of Ichadon
Dongcheon-dong, Gyeongju
Unified Silla, 817 / 818 CE
H. 106. cm

134
Roof Tile with Inscription: "興"
Sajeong-dong, Gyeongju
Unified Silla
L. 10.7 cm

135
Roof-end Tiles
Sajeong-dong, Gyeongju
Silla-Unified Silla
D. 15.3 cm (top left)

136
Bodhisattva Head
Hwangnyongsa Temple Site (presumed), Gyeongju
Silla, 7th century CE
H. 8.3 cm

137
Roof-end Tiles with Lotus Design
Hwangnyongsa Temple Site, Gyeongju
Silla-Unified Silla
D. 18.5 cm (bottom right)

138
Chimi (Ridge-end Roof Tile)
Hwangnyongsa Temple Site, Gyeongju
Silla
H. 182.0 cm

139
Stone Cover of the Sarira Chamber
Central Foundation Stone of the Wooden Pagoda Site at Hwangnyongsa Temple, Gyeongju
Silla, 645 CE
L. 44.3 cm

140
Sarira Outer Casket (North Side)
Central Foundation Stone of the Wooden Pagoda Site at Hwangnyongsa Temple, Gyeongju
Silla, 645 CE
L. 26.0 cm

141
Silver Plates with Inscriptions from the "Ye Dhamma Formular"
Central Foundation Stone of the Wooden Pagoda Site at Hwangnyongsa Temple, Gyeongju
Unified Silla
L. 8.0 cm (left)

142
Sarira Reliquaries
Wooden Pagoda Site at Hwangnyongsa Temple, Gyeongju
Silla-Unified Silla
H. 13.6 cm (bronze bowl with lid)

143
Silver Bowl with Lid
Central Foundation Stone of the Wooden Pagoda Site at Hwangnyongsa Temple, Gyeongju
Silla-Unified Silla
H. 4.5 cm

144
Octagonal Sarira Case
Central Foundation Stone of the Wooden Pagoda Site at Hwangnyongsa Temple, Gyeongju
Unified Silla
H. 12.3 cm

145
Square Case · Cylindrical Case
Central Foundation Stone of the Wooden Pagoda Site at Hwangnyongsa Temple, Gyeongju
Silla-Unified Silla
H. 6.1 cm (left)

146
Octagonal Sarira Case
Central Foundation Stone of the Wooden Pagoda Site at Hwangnyongsa Temple, Gyeongju
Unified Silla
D. 10.0 cm (left)

147
Lotus-shaped Pedestal
Central Foundation Stone of the Wooden Pagoda
Site at Hwangnyongsa Temple, Gyeongju
Silla-Unified Silla
H. 3.0 cm

148
Roof Tiles with Inscription: "令妙寺(靈廟寺)"
Gyeongju
Goryeo
L. 19.0 cm

149
Roof-end Tile with Human Face Design
Yeongmyosa Temple site, Gyeongju
Unified Silla
L. 11.5 cm
Treasure

150
Stone Lion
Bunhwangsa Temple, Gyeongju
Unified Silla, 8th century CE
H. 85.0 cm

151
Sarira Casket
Stone Brick Pagoda at Bunhwangsa Temple, Gyeongju
Silla, 634 CE
Total H. 72.0 cm

152
Ornaments
Stone Brick Pagoda at Bunhwangsa Temple, Gyeongju
Silla-Unified Silla
L. 25.7 cm (bottom left)

153
Sarira Reliquaries
Stone Brick Pagoda at Bunhwangsa Temple, Gyeongju
Silla, 645 CE-Goryeo 12th century CE
L. 8.4 cm (top right)

154
Brick with *Go* Board Design
Bunhwangsa Temple, Gyeongju
Unified Silla
L. 43.0 cm
Gyeongju National Research Institute of Cultural Heritage

155
Necklace
Cheonbu-dong, Ulleung
Unified Silla, 7th-8th century CE
D. 0.7-1.2 cm

156
Silla Style Pottery
Chodang-dong, Gangneung
Three Kingdoms, 6th century CE
H. 30.3 cm (back row, center)

157
Geumgwan Gaya Style Pottery
Samgye-dong, Gimhae
Three Kingdoms, 6th century CE
H. 28.0 cm (back row, center)

158
Silla Style Pottery
Samgye-dong, Gimhae
Three Kingdoms, 6th century CE
H. 25.7 cm (back row, center)

159
Dae Gaya Style Pottery
Jisan-dong, Goryeong
Three Kingdoms, 6th century CE
H. 21.5 cm (far left)

160
Silla Style Pottery
Jisan-dong, Goryeong
Three Kingdoms, 6th century CE
H. 28.9 cm (back row, center)

161
Excavated Artifacts from Nuam-ri Tomb
Nuam-ri, Chungju
Silla, 6th century CE
H. 16.8 cm (bottom left)

162
Excavated Artifacts from Seongdong-ri Tomb
Seongdong-ri, Paju
Silla, 6th century CE
H. 31.2 cm (back row, center)

163
Stele of the Tomb of King Munmu
Dongbu-dong, Gyeongju
(Discovered in 2009)
Unified Silla, 681-682 CE
H. 60.0 cm

164
Stele of the Tomb of King Munmu (bottom part)
Dongbu-dong, Gyeongju
(Discovered in 1961)
Unified Silla, 681-682 CE
H. 55.1 cm

165
Zodiac Figure (Pig)
Tomb Attributed to Kim Yu-sin
Unified Silla, 7th-8th century CE
H. 40.8 cm

166
Green-glazed Tile with Guardian Deity
Sacheonwangsa Temple Site, Gyeongju
Unified Silla, Around 679 CE
H. 90.0 cm
Gyeongju National Research Institute of Cultural Heritage

167
Green-glazed Tile with Guardian Deity
Sacheonwangsa Temple Site, Gyeongju
Unified Silla, Around 679 CE
H. 90.0 cm
Gyeongju National Research Institute of Cultural Heritage

168
Roof Tiles with Inscription: "四天王寺"
Sacheonwangsa Temple Site, Gyeongju
Unified Silla-Goryeo
L. 25.0 cm (back row, right)

169
Green-glazed Bricks
Sacheonwangsa Temple Site, Gyeongju
Unified Silla
L. 28.0 cm (top)
Gyeongju National Research Institute of Cultural Heritage

170
Roof-end Tiles
Sacheonwangsa Temple Site, Gyeongju
Unified Silla-Goryeo
W. 27.0 cm (back row, right)
Gyeongju National Research Institute of Cultural Heritage

171
Outer Sarira Casket · Inner Sarira Casket · Sarira Bottle
West Three-story Stone Pagoda at Gameunsa Temple Site, Gyeongju
Unified Silla, Around 682 CE
H. 16.5 cm (inner casket)
Treasure

172
Outer Sarira Casket
West Three-story Stone Pagoda at Gameunsa Temple Site, Gyeongju
Unified Silla, Around 682 CE
H. 28.0 cm
Treasure

173
Divine Bell of King Seongdeok the Great
Bongdeoksa Temple, Gyeongju
Unified Silla, 771 CE
H. 365.8 cm
National Treasure

174
Vajrapani
Seokguram Grotto, Gyeongju
Unified Silla, 8th century CE
H. 55.0 cm

175
Inner Sarira Casket (Records of the Construction and Renovation of the Wooden Pagoda at Hwangnyongsa Temple)
Central Foundation Stone of the Wooden Pagoda Site at Hwangnyongsa Temple, Gyeongju
Unified Silla, 872 CE
L. 22.5 cm (each)

176
Inner Sarira Casket Lid
Central Foundation Stone of the Wooden Pagoda Site at Hwangnyongsa Temple, Gyeongju
Unified Silla, 872 CE
L. 27.0 cm

177
Sarira Reliquary with Inscription: "仲和三年"
Wooden Pagoda Site at Hwangnyongsa Temple, Gyeongju
Unified Silla, 883 CE
H. 17.0 cm

178
Hip-end Roof Tile with Lotus Design
Hwangnyongsa Temple Site, Gyeongju
Unified Silla
L. 45.7 cm

179
Brick with Floral Medallion Design
Temple Site to the West of Hwangnyongsa Temple, Gyeongju
Unified Silla
L. 33.5 cm
Gyeongju National Research Institute of Cultural Heritage

180
Bricks with Floral Medallion and Dragon Design
Hwangnyongsa Temple Site, Gyeongju
Unified Silla
L. 36.8 cm

181
Eight Legions (Garuda and Kinnara)
Changrimsa Temple Site, Gyeongju
Unified Silla, 9th century CE
H. 88.0 cm (right)

182
Roof Tiles with Inscription: "昌林寺"
Changrimsa Temple Site · Cheongwansa Temple Site, Gyeongju
Unified Silla-Goryeo
L. 17.5 cm (right)
Gyeongju National Research Institute of Cultural Heritage

183
Brick with Buddha Design
Gapsansa Temple Site, Gyeongju
Unified Silla
L. 8.6 cm

184
Roof Tiles with Inscription: "甲山寺"
Gabsansa Temple Site, Gyeongju
Goryeo
L. 27.7 cm (right)

185
Small Votive Pagodas
Temple Site in Inwang-dong, Gyeongju
Unified Silla, 8th century CE
H. 10.8 cm (right)
Gyeongju National Research Institute of Cultural Heritage

186
Stone-carved Sutra
Chilbulam Temple, Gyeongju
Unified Silla
L. 12.0 cm

187
Sarira Case
Dongcheon-dong, Gyeongju
Unified Silla, 9th century CE
H. 9.3 cm

188
Sutra Case
Namsan Mountain (presumed), Gyeongju
Unified Silla
H. 3.9 cm

189
Infant Buddha
Nonsan
Silla, 7th century CE
H. 10.7 cm

190
Pensive Bodhisattva
Seonggeon-dong, Gyeongju
Silla, 7th century CE
H. 14.1 cm

191
Pensive Bodhisattva
Songhwasan Mountain, Gyeongju
Silla, 7th century CE
H. 125.0 cm

192
Maitreya Triad
Jangchanggok Valley, Namsan Mountain, Gyeongju
Silla, 7th century CE
H. 167.0 cm (center)
Treasure

193
Buddhist Plaques (Buddha Triad, Bodhisattva)
Donggung Palace and Wolji Pond, Gyeongju
Unified Silla, 7th century CE
H. 21.3 cm (top)
Treasure

194
Buddha Triad
Donggung Palace and Wolji Pond, Gyeongju
Unified Silla, late 7th century CE
H. 27.0 cm
Treasure

195
Buddha
Provenance Unknown
Unified Silla, 8th century CE
H. 22.3 cm

196
Buddha
Provenance Unknown
Unified Silla, 8th century CE
H. 21.6 cm

197
Buddha
Provenance Unknown
Unified Silla, 9th century CE
H. 29.0 cm

198
Buddhas
Donggung Palace and Wolji Pond, Gyeongju
Unified Silla, Late 8th century CE
H. 35.0 cm (right)

199
Buddhas
Donggung Palace and Wolji Pond, Gyeongju
Unified Silla, 8th-9th century CE
H. 21.0 cm (top left)

200
Vairocana Buddha
Provenance Unknown
Unified Silla, 8th century CE
H. 39.7 cm

201
Vairocana Buddha
Provenance Unknown
Unified Silla, 9th century CE
H. 31.5 cm

202
Bhaishajyaguru Buddha
Baengnyulsa Temple, Gyeongju
Unified Silla, about 800 CE
H. 179.0 cm
National Treasure

203
Bodhisattva
Dong-gu, Daegu
Unified Silla, 8th century CE
H. 11.7 cm

204
Bodhisattva
Sangju
Unified Silla, 8th century CE
H. 13.0 cm

205
Eleven-faced Avalokiteshvara
Nangsan Mountain, Gyeongju
Unified Silla, 8th century CE
H. 200.0 cm

206
Buddhist Ornamental Plaques
Donggung Palace and Wolji Pond, Gyeongju
Unified Silla, 8th century CE
L. 4.0-10.0 cm

207
Buddha
Inwang-dong, Gyeongju
Silla, 7th century CE
H. 112.0 cm

208
Bhaishajyaguru Buddha
Nangsan Mountain, Gyeongju
Unified Silla
H. 128.5 cm

209
Buddha
Wangjeonggok Valley, Namsan Mountain, Gyeongju
Unified Silla, 8th century CE
H. 201.0 cm

210
Buddha
Gyeongjueupseong Walled Town, Gyeongju
Unified Silla, 8th century CE
H. 175.0 cm

211
Buddha
Osangye Valley, Namsan Mountain, Gyeongju
Unified Silla, 9th century CE
H. 172.7 cm

212
Bhaishajyaguru Buddha
Yongjanggok Valley, Namsan Mountain, Gyeongju
Unified Silla, late 8th-9th century CE
H. 305.0 cm

213
Avalokiteshvara Bodhisattva
Nangsan Mountain, Gyeongju
Unified Silla, 9th century CE
H. 376.0 cm

214
Buddha Head
Cheolwagol Valley, Namsan Mountain, Gyeongju
Unified Silla, late 8th-early 9th century CE
H. 153.0 cm

215
Vajrapanis
Ha-dong, Gyeongju
Unified Silla
H. 84.0 cm

216
Vajrapanis
Temple Site in Guhwang-dong, Gyeongju
Unified Silla, 7th century CE
H. 143.0 cm (left)

217
Four Heavenly Kings
Gyeongjueupseong Walled Town, Gyeongju
Unified Silla, 8th century CE
H. 83.0 cm

218
Three-story Stone Pagoda
Goseonsa Temple Site, Gyeongju
Unified Silla, Before 686 CE
H. 10.1 m
National Treasure

219
Three-story Stone Pagoda
Seungsogol Valley, Namsan Mountain, Gyeongju
Unified Silla, 9th century CE
H. 377.0 cm

220
Three-story Stone Pagoda
Samneung, Namsan Mountain, Gyeongju
Unified Silla
H. 216.0 cm

221
Stone Lantern
Gyeongjueupseong Walled Town, Gyeongju
Unified Silla, 8th-9th century CE
H. 259.0 cm

222
Stone Lantern
Gyeongjueupseong Walled Town, Gyeongju
Unified Silla, 8th-9th century CE
H. 221.0 cm

223
Sarira Reliquaries-Sarira Jar · Sarira Bottle · Votive Pagodas
East Three-story Stone Pagoda at Seodong-ri, Bonghwa
Unified Silla, 9th century CE
H. 9.1 cm (jar)

224
Sarira Reliquaries-Votive Pagoda · Sarira Jar · Sutra Case
Three-story Stone Pagoda at the Chukseosa Temple, Bonghwa
Unified Silla, 867 CE
L. 24.1 cm (front)

225
Sarira Reliquaries-Sarira Jars · Pagoda Stone Tablet Records
Three-story Stone Pagoda at the Beopgwangsa Temple Site, Pohang
Unified Silla, 9th century CE
H. 10.8 cm (far right)

226
Clay Figure
Yonggang-dong, Gyeongju
Unified Silla, 8th century CE
H. 17.1 cm

227
Belt Pieces
Donggung Palace and Wolji Pond, Gyeongju
Unified Silla
L. 5.4 cm (far left)

228
Official Seal
376, Hwangnam-dong, Gyeongju
Unified Silla
L. 3.2 cm

229
Official Seal
681-1, Dongcheon-dong, Gyeongju
Unified Silla
L. 3.5 cm

230
Wooden Slip Document
Donggung Palace and Wolji Pond, Gyeongju
Unified Silla, 8th-9th century CE
L. 31.9 cm

231
Inkstones
Gyeongju
Unified Silla
H. 10.2 cm (top right)

232
Lacquerware Inkstone
Donggung Palace and Wolji Pond, Gyeongju
Unified Silla, 8th-9th century CE
L. 15.0 cm

233
Inkstone with Inscription: "椋司"
Donggung Palace and Wolji Pond, Gyeongju
Unified Silla, 8th-9th century CE
D. 16.5 cm

234
Large Jar with Inscription: "十石入瓮"
Donggung Palace and Wolji Pond, Gyeongju
Unified Silla, 8th century CE
H. 150.0 cm

235
Pottery and Wooden Tools Excavated from an Well
Inwang-dong, Gyeongju
Unified Silla
L. 29.5 cm (front row bucket)

236
Wooden Slip with Inscription
Inwang-dong, Gyeongju
Unified Silla
L. 24.1 cm

237
Comb
Inwang-dong, Gyeongju
Unified Silla
L. 10.3 cm

238
Dog Bones
Hwangnam-dong, Gyeongju
Unified Silla
L. 18.1 cm (far left)

239
Bronze Vessels · Bronze Spoon · Bronze Hairpins
Inwang-dong, Gyeongju
Unified Silla
D. 7.0 cm (dish)

240
Pottery with Inscription: "辛審龍王"
Donggung Palace and Wolji Pond, Gyeongju
Unified Silla, 8th-9th century CE
D. 19.9 cm

241
Pottery with Inscription: "辛審龍王"
Donggung Palace and Wolji Pond, Gyeongju
Unified Silla, 8th-9th century CE
D. 11.4 cm

242
Censer Lid
Donggung Palace and Wolji Pond, Gyeongju
Unified Silla, 8th-9th century CE
H. 16.5 cm

243
Scissors
Donggung Palace and Wolji Pond, Gyeongju
Unified Silla, 8th-9th century CE
L. 7.3 cm (bottom)

244
Scissors
Donggung Palace and Wolji Pond, Gyeongju
Unified Silla, 8th-9th century CE
L. 13.0 cm (top center)

245
Round Plates
Donggung Palace and Wolji Pond, Gyeongju
Unified Silla, 8th-9th century CE
D. 12.5 cm (top left)

246
Roof-end Tile with Lotus Design
Donggung Palace and Wolji Pond, Gyeongju
Unified Silla, late 7th century CE
D. 13.3 cm

247
Roof Tile with Inscription: "儀鳳四年皆土"
Donggung Palace and Wolji Pond, Gyeongju
Unified Silla, 679 CE
L. 39.2 cm

248
Roof-end Tiles
Gyeongju
Unified Silla
L. 35.3 cm (top right)

249
Roof-end Tiles with Lotus Design
Hwangnyongsa Temple Site, Gyeongju · Heungnyunsa Temple Site (presumed), Gyeongju
Unified Silla
D. 13.2 cm (right)

250
Roof-end Tiles with Animal Design
Donggung Palace and Wolji Pond, Gyeongju
Unified Silla, 8th-9th century CE
D. 14.2 cm (left)

251
Roof-end Tile with Inscription: "在城"
Donggung Palace and Wolji Pond, Gyeongju
Unified Silla, 8th-9th century CE
D. 16.9 cm

252
Roof-end Tiles and Roof Tiles with Inscription: "在城"
Donggung Palace and Wolji Pond, Gyeongju
Unified Silla, 8th-9th century CE
D. 15.5 cm (left)

253
Brick with Dragon and Building Designs
Temple Site in Jungsan-dong, Ulsan
Unified Silla
L. 15.4 cm

254
Brick with Building Design
Temple Site in Jungsan-dong, Ulsan
Unified Silla, 8th century CE
L. 20.0 cm

255
Padlock with Inscription: "東宮衙鎰"
Donggung Palace and Wolji Pond, Gyeongju
Unified Silla, 8th-9th century CE
L. 32.3 cm

256
Wooden Slip with Inscription: "奉太子君"
Donggung Palace and Wolji Pond, Gyeongju
Unified Silla, 8th-9th century CE
L. 6.1 cm

257
Brick with Inscription: "調露二年"
Donggung Palace and Wolji Pond, Gyeongju
Unified Silla, 680 CE
W. 32.3 cm

258
Jar with Lid
Donggung Palace and Wolji Pond, Gyeongju
Unified Silla, 7th century CE
H. 15.7 cm (jar)

259
Kaiyuan Tongbao Coins
Donggung Palace and Wolji Pond, Gyeongju
Unified Silla, 7th century CE
D. 2.5 cm (bottom)

260
Roof-end Tiles
Donggung Palace and Wolji Pond, Gyeongju
Unified Silla, 7th century CE
D. 12.5 cm (convex roof-end tile)

261
Tile with Lotus Design and Green Glaze
Donggung Palace and Wolji Pond, Gyeongju
Unified Silla, 7th century CE
D. 12.9 cm

262
Roof Tile with Beast Design and Green Glaze
Donggung Palace and Wolji Pond, Gyeongju
Unified Silla, late 7th century CE
H. 29.2 cm

263
Roof-end Tile with Lotus Design
Donggung Palace and Wolji Pond, Gyeongju
Unified Silla, 7th century CE
D. 14.0 cm

264
Roof-end Tile with Lotus and Floral Medallion Design
Donggung Palace and Wolji Pond, Gyeongju
Unified Silla, 7th century CE
D. 15.0 cm

265
Roof-end Tile with Lotus and Floral Medallion Design
Donggung Palace and Wolji Pond, Gyeongju
Unified Silla, 7th century CE
D. 13.8 cm

266
Roof-end Tile with Honeysuckle and Floral Medallion Design
Donggung Palace and Wolji Pond, Gyeongju
Unified Silla, 7th century CE
D. 14.5 cm

267
Roof-end Tile with Lotus Design
Donggung Palace and Wolji Pond, Gyeongju
Unified Silla, 8th century CE
D. 12.8 cm

268
Roof-end Tile with Lotus Design
Donggung Palace and Wolji Pond, Gyeongju
Unified Silla, 8th century CE
D. 12.0 cm

269
Roof-end Tile with Lotus Design
Donggung Palace and Wolji Pond, Gyeongju
Unified Silla, 8th century CE
D. 14.0 cm

270
Roof-end Tile with Floral Medallion Design
Donggung Palace and Wolji Pond, Gyeongju
Unified Silla, 8th century CE
D. 15.4 cm

271
Roof-end Tile with Floral Medallion Design
Donggung Palace and Wolji Pond, Gyeongju
Unified Silla, 8th century CE
D. 11.0 cm

272
Roof-end Tile with Lotus and Arabesque Design
Donggung Palace and Wolji Pond, Gyeongju
Unified Silla, 9th-10th century CE
D. 13.0 cm

273
Bricks
Donggung Palace and Wolji Pond, Gyeongju
Unified Silla, late 7th-8th century CE
L. 32.0 cm (front)

274
Door Handle with Floral Medallion Design
Donggung Palace and Wolji Pond, Gyeongju
Unified Silla, 8th-9th century CE
Handle D. 13.5 cm

275
Door Handles with Bestial Face Design
Donggung Palace and Wolji Pond, Gyeongju
Unified Silla, 8th-9th century CE
L. 10.4 cm (left)

276
Lotus Bud Ornaments
Donggung Palace and Wolji Pond, Gyeongju
Unified Silla, late 7th-9th century CE
H. 18.8 cm (right)

277
End Ornament with Arabesque Design
Donggung Palace and Wolji Pond, Gyeongju
Unified Silla, late 7th-9th century CE
D. 8.1 cm

278
End Ornament with Arabesque Design
Donggung Palace and Wolji Pond, Gyeongju
Unified Silla, late 7th-9th century CE
W. 17.3 cm

279
Wind Chime
Donggung Palace and Wolji Pond, Gyeongju
Unified Silla, late 7th-9th century CE
H. 16.0 cm

280
Window Shade Ornaments
Donggung Palace and Wolji Pond, Gyeongju
Unified Silla, late 7th-9th century CE
L. 18.0-20.2 cm

281
Decorative Wall Hooks
Donggung Palace and Wolji Pond, Gyeongju
Unified Silla, late 7th-9th century CE
L. 8.3-8.5 cm

282
Dragon Head Decoration
Donggung Palace and Wolji Pond, Gyeongju
Unified Silla, 8th-9th century CE
L. 16.4 cm

283
Phoenix-shaped Decoration
Donggung Palace and Wolji Pond, Gyeongju
Unified Silla, 8th-9th century CE
H. 10.6 cm

284
Juryeonggu
Donggung Palace and Wolji Pond, Gyeongju
Unified Silla, late 7th-9th century CE
H. 4.8 cm
Replica

285
Boat
Donggung Palace and Wolji Pond, Gyeongju
Unified Silla, late 7th-9th century CE
L. 620.0 cm

286
Bowls
Donggung Palace and Wolji Pond, Gyeongju
Unified Silla, late 7th-9th century CE
D. 15.1 cm (top left)

287
Bowl with Lid
Donggung Palace and Wolji Pond, Gyeongju
Unified Silla, late 7th-9th century CE
H. 11.2 cm

288
Dishes
Donggung Palace and Wolji Pond, Gyeongju
Unified Silla, late 7th-9th century CE
D. 19.7 cm (upper left)

289
Spoons
Donggung Palace and Wolji Pond, Gyeongju
Unified Silla, 8th-9th century CE
L. 26.7 cm (far right)

290
Ladles
Donggung Palace and Wolji Pond, Gyeongju
Unified Silla, 8th-9th century CE
L. 23.0 cm (far left)

291
Lacquerware Vessels
Donggung Palace and Wolji Pond, Gyeongju
Unified Silla, 8th-9th century CE
H. 4.7 cm (left)

292
Lacquerware Vessels
Donggung Palace and Wolji Pond, Gyeongju
Unified Silla, 8th-9th century CE
H. 6.1 cm (left)

293
Portable Hearth
Donggung Palace and Wolji Pond, Gyeongju
Unified Silla, 8th-9th century CE
H. 19.5 cm

294
Steamer
Donggung Palace and Wolji Pond, Gyeongju
Unified Silla, 8th-9th century CE
H. 32.8 cm

295
Bowl with Ink-painted Designs
Donggung Palace and Wolji Pond, Gyeongju
Unified Silla, 8th-9th century CE
D. 11.3 cm

296
Bowl with a Human Face Motif
Donggung Palace and Wolji Pond, Gyeongju
Unified Silla, 8th-9th century CE
H. 4.9 cm

297
Lids with Stamped Design
Donggung Palace and Wolji Pond, Gyeongju
Unified Silla, 8th-9th century CE
H. 5.5 cm (left bottom)

298
Bottles with Stamped Design
Donggung Palace and Wolji Pond, Gyeongju
Unified Silla, 8th-9th century CE
H. 11.0 cm (right)

299
Bottle with Stamped Design
Donggung Palace and Wolji Pond, Gyeongju
Unified Silla, 8th-9th century CE
H. 15.5 cm

300
Pottery with Stamped Design
Donggung Palace and Wolji Pond, Gyeongju
Unified Silla, 8th-9th century CE
H. 36.3 cm (right)

301
Pottery Vessels
Donggung Palace and Wolji Pond, Gyeongju
Unified Silla, 9th-10th century CE
H. 87.7 cm (right)

302
Comb
Donggung Palace and Wolji Pond, Gyeongju
Unified Silla, 8th-9th century CE
L. 9.7 cm

303
Hair Part Tools
Donggung Palace and Wolji Pond, Gyeongju
Unified Silla, 8th-9th century CE
L. 14.5 cm (left)

304
Hairpins
Donggung Palace and Wolji Pond, Gyeongju
Unified Silla, 8th-9th century CE
L. 9.0 cm (far right)

305
Rings
Donggung Palace and Wolji Pond, Gyeongju
Unified Silla, 8th-9th century CE
D. 2.0 cm (right)

306
Hairpin
Donggung Palace and Wolji Pond, Gyeongju
Unified Silla, 8th-9th century CE
L. 15.6 cm

307
Gold Ornaments
Donggung Palace and Wolji Pond, Gyeongju
Unified Silla, 8th-9th century CE
L. 4.5 cm (nail)

308
Glass Beads
Donggung Palace and Wolji Pond, Gyeongju
Unified Silla, 8th-9th century CE
D. 0.7-4.7 cm

309
Clay Figures
Yonggang-dong, Gyeongju
Unified Silla, 8th century CE
H. 14.0 cm (front left)

310
Female Clay Figurine
Hwangseong-dong, Gyeongju
Silla, 7th century CE
H. 16.5 cm

311
Male Clay Figurine
Yonggang-dong, Gyeongju
Unified Silla, 8th century CE
H. 17.4 cm

312
Zodiac Figure (Monkey)
Tomb of King Seongdeok, Joyang-dong, Gyeongju
Unified Silla, 8th century CE
H. 116.0 cm

313
Zodiac Figures
Hwagok-ri, Goryeong
Unified Silla, 9th century CE
H. 12.0-15.0 cm

314
Soapstone Zodiac Figures
Tomb Attributed to King Minae Mangseong-ri, Gyeongju
Unified Silla, 8th-9th century CE
H. 8.0-11.1 cm

315
Zodiac Figures
Temple Site in Hagu-ri, Gyeongju
Unified Silla, 9th-10th century CE
H. 42.0-45.0 cm

316
Zodiac Figures
Gyeongju · Provenance Unknown
Unified Silla
H. 106.0 cm (left)

317
Four Heavenly Kings
Gyeongju
Unified Silla
H. 95.0 cm (right)

318
Stone Door Inscribed with Guardian Deity Figure
Stone-chamber Tomb in Seoak-dong, Gyoengju
Unified Silla
H. 150.0 cm

319
Stone Lion
Gyo-dong, Gyeongju
Unified Silla
H. 65.0 cm

320
Stone Lion
Provenance Unknown
Unified Silla
H. 98.0 cm

321
Cremation Urn with Inscription: "元和十年"
Tomb Attributed to King Minae
Mangseong-ri, Gyeongju
Unified Silla, 815 CE
H. 19.3 cm

322
Green-glazed Cremation Urns
Namsan Mountain, Gyeongju
Unified Silla, Estimated 8th century CE
H. 39.0 cm (left)

323
House-shaped Cremation Urn
Bukgun-dong, Gyeongju
Unified Silla, 8th century CE
H. 43.4 cm

324
Cremation Urn and Lid
Seokjang-dong, Gyeongju
Unified Silla
H. 23.5 cm

325
Cremation Urn with Lid
Nawon-ri, Gyeongju
Unified Silla
H. 13.8 cm

326
Cremation Urns
Gyeongju region
Unified Silla, 8th-10th century CE
H. 27.0 cm (back row, far right)

327
Gilt-bronze Shoes
North Mound of
Hwangnamdaechong, Gyeongju
Silla, 5th century CE
L. 27.5 cm

328
Gilt-bronze Shoes
Geumgwanchong Tomb, Gyeongju
Silla, 5th century CE
L. 30.5 cm (top)

329
Silver Bowl with Lid
South Mound of
Hwangnamdaechong Tomb,
Gyeongju
Silla, 5th century CE
H. 16.8 cm

330
Lead-glazed Jar
Wolseong-ro Ga-5 Tomb, Gyeongju
Silla, 5th-6th century CE
H. 11.0 cm

331
Bronze Mirror
South Mound of
Hwangnamdaechong Tomb,
Gyeongju
Silla, 5th century CE
D. 15.5 cm

332
Tri-colored Glazed Cremation Urn
Joyang-dong, Gyeongju
Unified Silla, 8th century CE
H. 16.5 cm

333
Celadon Bowl
Donggung Palace and Wolji Pond,
Gyeongju
Tang Dynasty, 9th century CE
D. 16.2 cm

334
Stone Bracelet
Wolseong-ro Ga-29 Tomb,
Gyeongju
Silla, 4th century CE
D. 8.3 cm

335
Harness Fittings
South Mound of
Hwangnamdaechong, Gyeongju
Silla, 5th century CE
H. 4.5 cm (left)

336
Japanese *Hajiki*-style Pottery
Wolseong-ro Ga-31 Tomb,
Gyeongju
Silla, 4th century CE
H. 12.6 cm (far right)

337
Candle Wick Scissors
Donggung Palace and Wolji Pond,
Gyeongju
Unified Silla, 8th century CE
L. 25.5 cm
Treasure

338
Deer Bone Decorations with Floral and Bird Designs
Donggung Palace and Wolji Pond,
Gyeongju
Unified Silla, 8th-9th century CE
L. 21.8 cm (far right)

339
Glassware
North Mound of
Hwangnamdaechong Tomb,
Gyeongju
Silla, 5th century CE
H. 7.6 cm

340
Glassware
Geumgwanchong Tomb, Gyeongju
Silla, 5th century CE
H. 9.2 cm

341
Glass Bowl
South Mound of Hwangnamdaechong Tomb, Gyeongju
Silla, 5th century CE
H. 6.7 cm

342
Glassware
North Mound of Hwangnamdaechong Tomb, Gyeongju
Silla, 5th century CE
H. 7.3 cm

343
Glassware
Cheonmachong Tomb, Gyeongju
Silla, 6th century CE
H. 7.4 cm
Treasure

344
Glass Pendant
Gyerim-ro Tomb 14, Gyeongju
Silla, 6th century CE
L. 4.9 cm

345
Harness Fittings
Gyerim-ro Tomb 14, Gyeongju
Silla, 6th century CE
L. 2.4 cm (far right)

346
Necklace with Inlaid Glass Bead
Tomb 4 of Michuwangneung Tomb District C, Gyeongju
Silla, 5th-6th century CE
L. 24.0 cm
Treasure

347
Golden Treasure Sword
Gyerim-ro Tomb 14, Gyeongju
Silla, before 6th century CE
L. 36.0 cm
Treasure

348
Drinking Horn and Stand
Tomb 7 of Michuwangneung Tomb District C, Gyeongju
Silla, 5th-6th century CE
H. 17.0 cm

349
Gilt bronze Drinking Horn
Geumgwanchong Tomb, Gyeongju
Silla, 5th century CE
L. 23.7 cm

350
Drinking Horn
Naengsu-ri, Pohang
Silla, 6th century CE
L. 27.8 cm

351
Corner Pillar
Square Tomb in Gujeong-dong, Gyeongju
Unified Silla, 9th-10th century CE
H. 73.6 cm

352
Stone with Lion and Peacock Designs
Gyeongju
Unified Silla, 8th century CE
L. 300.0 cm

353
Portrait of King Gyeongsun
Empire of Korea, 1904 CE
Painting on Silk
152.5 × 87.5 cm
Collection at Sunghyejeon Shrine

354
Bottle with Flattened Sides and Bottles with Incised Line Pattern
Cheonghaejin, Wando
Unified Silla
H. 32.7cm (left)

355
Portrait of Choi Chiwon
Joseon, 1793 CE
Painting on Silk
140.0 × 100.0 cm
Collection of the Gyeongju Choi Clan

356
Sarira Reliquaries (Sarira Bottle, Sarira Casket, Rings, Beads)
Three-story Stone Pagoda at the Seungansa Temple Site, Hamyang
Goryeo, 10th century CE
D. 8.5 cm (sarira casket)

357
Buddhist Ritual Offering Implements from Mangdeoksa Temple Site
Mangdeoksa Temple site, Gyeongju
Goryeo
H. 33.0 cm (vase)

358
Bronze Gong
Gulbulsa Temple Site, Gyeongju
Goryeo, 1183 CE
L. 33.6 cm

Permanent Exhibition Guide Book of the
Gyeongju National Museum

History and Culture of Silla

Editor
Lee Je-hyun, Yang Hee-chung, Kim Hyun-hee

Contributor
Kim Dae-hwan, Kim Hyun-hee, Lee Hyun-tae, Lee Je-hyun
Shin Myung-hee, Yang Hee-chung, Yoon Sang-deok(Alphabetical order)

Proofreader
Lee Je-hyun, Yang Hee-chung, Lee Jun-hyeok
Shin Hyun-woo, Sohn Jong-eun, Son Su-yeon, Yoon Seo-young

Photography
Kim Kwang-seop, Shin sung-jIn(K-art Studio), Oh Se-yoon

Translator
Ko Il-Hong

English Editor
Pillip Maher

Design and Production
Design Play with Dreams
12-9 Seoae-ro 5-gil, Jung-gu, Seoul, Korea 4623
T. +82-2-2279-3986

Printing
Nanumprinting Co, Ltd.

First Published
Octorber 1, 2025

ISBN
979-11-88648-36-8 93910

Publication Registration Number
11-1371081-100003-01

Price
35,000KRW